Tiantian Zhongwen Graded Chinese Readers

天天中文

Bicycle Kingdom
and other stories

TURQUOISE LEVEL

MACMILLAN

目 录
Contents

1

盲人的灯笼
The Blind Man's Lantern

帮助别人，也是帮助自己。如果你经常帮助别人，
当你需要帮助的时候，别人也会帮助你。

盲人 *n.*
blind person

提 *v.*
carry

明亮 *adj.*
bright

Yǒu yí gè mángrén, tā měi cì wǎnshang chūqù de shíhou,
有 一 个 盲人， 他 每 次 晚上 出去 的 时候，

shǒu li zǒngshì tízhe yí gè míngliàng de dēnglong. Biérén kànle
手 里 总是 提着 一 个 明亮 的 灯笼。 别人 看了

juéde hěn qíguài, jiù wèn tā: "Nǐ zìjǐ kànbujiàn, wèishénme hái
觉得 很 奇怪， 就 问 他："你 自己 看不见， 为什么 还

yào tízhe dēnglong zǒulù ne?"
要 提着 灯笼 走路 呢?"

　　Mángrén xiàozhe shuō: "Wǒ zìjǐ kànbujiàn, dànshì, wǒ de
　　盲人 笑着 说:"我 自己 看不见,但是,我 的

dēnglong kěyǐ zhàoliàng biérén ya."
灯笼 可以 照亮 别人 呀。"

　　"Zhàoliàng biérén, gēn nǐ yǒu shénme guānxì ne?"
　　"照亮 别人,跟 你 有 什么 关系 呢?"

　　Mángrén shuō: "Wǒ tízhe dēnglong bú shì wèi zìjǐ zhàolù,
　　盲人 说:"我 提着 灯笼 不 是 为 自己 照路,

ér shì wèile ràng biérén kàndào wǒ. Zhèyàng, tāmen jiù bú huì
而 是 为了 让 别人 看到 我。这样,他们 就 不 会

zhuàngdào wǒ le."
撞到 我 了。"

| 灯笼 *n.* |
| lantern |
| 奇怪 *adj.* |
| weird |
| 照亮 *v.* |
| light, illuminate |
| 撞 *v.* |
| bump into |

想一想 Questions

你觉得盲人聪明不聪明? 为什么?

盲人为什么要提灯笼?

语言点 Language Points

跟……（没）有
关系
have something/
nothing to do with

1. 照亮别人，跟你有什么关系呢？

Why does lighting the way for others have anything to do with you?

"跟……（没）有关系"中的"关系"是名词，表示人或事物之间的某种联系。

In the phrase "跟……（没）有关系"，"关系" is a noun to show the relationship between people or things.

（1）我今天迟到，跟昨天睡觉晚有很大关系。

（2）考试成绩跟学习时间、学习兴趣有很大关系。

就
will

2. 这样，他们就不会撞到我了。

This way, they will not bump into me.

"就"，副词，表示承接上文情况，得出结论。

"就" is an adverb that introduces a conclusion on the basis of the previous sentence(s).

（1）没事儿就回家吧，好好休息休息。

（2）有他参加就好，我最喜欢听他唱歌了。

练 习 | Exercises

判断正误　True (T) or false (F)

(1) 盲人每天晚上都提灯笼出去。　　　　　　（　　）

(2) 盲人总是在白天提着灯笼。　　　　　　　（　　）

(3) 盲人提灯笼，是怕别人看不见路。　　　　（　　）

文化略观 | Cultural Insights

红灯笼
Red Lanterns

　　在中国，灯笼除了照明之外，还有很多其他的含义。早在汉朝，每年的元宵节前后，家家户户就挂起红灯笼，以此营造红火、喜庆的气氛。后来，红灯笼就成了团圆、兴旺、富贵的象征。喜庆的日子，人们都喜欢挂起红红的灯笼。尤其是在海外华人聚居区，比如唐人街，一年四季都挂着大红灯笼。

Apart from lighting the way, lanterns have many uses in China. As early as the Han Dynasty, people hung red lanterns during the Lantern Festival to create an atmosphere of lively festivity. Later, red lanterns gradually became tokens of reunion, prosperity and wealth, dignity and fortune. On festive occasions, everyone likes to hang bright red lanterns. In many overseas Chinese residential areas, like Chinatowns, scarlet lanterns are hung all year around.

2 汉语发音
Pronouncing Chinese

现在越来越多的外国人开始学习汉语。
有的人觉得汉语的发音很难。你觉得呢?

我能问(吻)你吗?

声调 n.
tone

超市 n.
supermarket

女士 n.
lady

Hànyǔ de fāyīn yǒudiǎnr nán. Wèishénme ne?
汉语 的 发音 有点儿 难。 为什么 呢?

Dì-yī, yīnwèi Hànyǔ yǒu sì gè shēngdiào. Wàiguórén
第一, 因为 汉语 有 四 个 声调。 外国人

juéde shēngdiào hěn nán, jīngcháng nào xiàohua. Yí cì, yí gè
觉得 声调 很 难, 经常 闹 笑话。 一 次, 一 个

wàiguórén zhǎo bú dào tā yào qù de nà jiā chāoshì. Tā kànjiàn
外国人 找 不 到 他 要 去 的 那 家 超市。 他 看见

pángbiān yǒu yí wèi piàoliang de nǚshì, jiù shuō: "Xiǎojiě, wǒ yǒu
旁边 有 一 位 漂亮 的 女士,就 说:"小姐, 我 有

yí gè wèntí, wǒ néng wèn nǐ ma?" Nà wèi nǚshì tīngle què
一 个 问题， 我 能 问 你 吗？" 那 位 女士 听了 却

fēicháng shēngqì. Nǐ zhīdào wèishénme ma? Yīnwèi nàge wàiguórén
非常 生气。 你 知道 为什么 吗？ 因为 那个 外国人

bǎ "wèn（wèn）" shuōchéngle "wěn（wěn）". Chúle shēngdiào
把 "wèn（问）" 说成了 "wěn（吻）"。 除了 声调

yǐwài, érhuàyīn yě bù róngyì. Bǐrúshuō, "xiǎohái" yào shuōchéng
以外， 儿化音 也 不 容易。 比如说， "小孩" 要 说成

"xiǎoháir".
"小孩儿"。

　　Dì-èr, juǎnshéyīn hěn nán. Bǐrúshuō, "wǒ shì（shì）Měiguórén",
　　第二， 卷舌音 很 难。 比如说，"我 是（shì） 美国人"，

yǒude liúxuéshēng shuōchéng "wǒ shì（sì）Měiguórén". Hái yǒu,
有的 留学生 说成 "我 是（sì） 美国人"。 还 有，

"sì" hé "shí" hěn duō rén yě fēn bù qīngchu. Suǒyǐ shàngkè de
"四" 和 "十" 很 多 人 也 分 不 清楚。 所以 上课 的

shíhou, lǎoshī ràng wǒmen shuō: sì shì sì, shí shì shí; shísì shì
时候， 老师 让 我们 说： 四 是 四， 十 是 十； 十四 是

shísì, sìshí shì sìshí.
十四， 四十 是 四十。

生气 *v.*	get angry
吻 *v.*	kiss
除了……以外	apart from
卷舌音 *n.*	retroflex sounds (made by curling the tongue)
分清楚	clearly distinguish
分 *v.*	distinguish
清楚 *adj.*	clear

想一想 **Questions**

那位 女士 为什么 很 生气？

你 觉得 "四" 和 "十" 的 发音 容易 吗？

语言点 Language Points

闹笑话
make a fool of
oneself

1. 外国人觉得声调很难，经常闹笑话。

Non-Chinese speakers feel it is difficult to learn tones, and often make fools of themselves.

"闹笑话"是指因粗心大意或缺乏知识经验而发生可笑的错误。

"闹笑话" means to make a fool of oneself because of carelessness or lack of knowledge and experience.

（1）不懂广东话的人刚到广东，常常会闹笑话。
（2）我刚来中国的时候，闹了不少笑话。

比如说
for example

2. 卷舌音很难。比如说，"我是（shì）美国人"，有的留学生说成"我是（sì）美国人"。

Retroflex sounds are very difficult. For example, some foreign students say "我是（sì）美国人" instead of "我是（shì）美国人".

"比如说"，用来引出说明某事物、某情况的例子。

The phrase "比如说" is used to introduce an example to illustrate something or certain circumstances.

（1）中国菜有很多种，比如说，四川菜、广东菜、山东菜等。
（2）我们班的同学来自很多不同的国家，比如说，日本、美国和英国。

练 习 | Exercises

判断正误　True (T) or false (F)

（1）外国人觉得汉语的声调很难。　　　　　　　　（　　）

（2）女士听了外国人的话很生气，因为她不想帮助他。　（　　）

（3）外国人说"四"和"十"时，发音可能是一样的。　（　　）

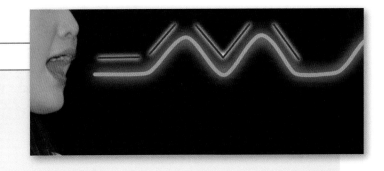

文化略观 | Cultural Insights

汉语的声调
The Tones of Chinese

　　汉语是有声调的语言，声调不同，意思就不同。因此，声调具有区别意义的作用。比如，mā（妈）、má（麻）、mǎ（马）、mà（骂）。

　　不同声调的汉字连在一起时，有时会出现变调。两个第三声的汉字连在一起时，前一个汉字的音调会变为第二声。比如，"你好（nǐhǎo）"的实际读音为"níhǎo"。

Chinese is a tonal language. Different tones produce different meanings. Thus, tones can be used to distinguish between meanings, such as mā (妈, mother), má (麻, hemp), mǎ (马, horse), mà (骂, curse).

When characters with different tones are used together, tone shift may occur. When two characters with the third tone are put together, the first character changes into the second tone. For example, "你好 (nǐhǎo)" is pronounced as "níhǎo".

3 | "好"的含意
The Meaning of "好"

你想过吗，"女"和"子"在一起，为什么就
组成（zǔchéng:compose）了"好"字？你是怎么记住汉字的？

有意思 *adj.*
interesting

Zhāng lǎoshī: Dàjiā xiǎng yì xiǎng, wèishénme "hǎo" zhège zì shì
张　老师：大家　想　一　想，为什么　"好"这个　字　是

"nǚ" hé "zǐ" zài yìqǐ ya?
"女"和"子"在　一起　呀？

Xuésheng : "Nǚzǐ" jiù shì nǚháizi, yǒule nǚpéngyou jiù shì
学生　　A："女子"就　是　女孩子，有了　女朋友　就　是

"hǎo".
"好"。

Xuésheng : Bú duì. "Nǚ" shì "nǚ'ér", "zǐ" shì "érzi", yòu
学生　　B：不　对。"女"是"女儿"，"子"是"儿子"，又

12

yǒu nǚ'ér yòu yǒu érzi jiù shì "hǎo".
有 女儿 又 有 儿子 就 是 "好"。

Xuésheng : Yě bú duì. "Nǚ" shì "nǚháir", "zǐ" shì
学生　　C：也 不 对。"女" 是 "女孩儿"，"子" 是

"nánháir", nǚháir hé nánháir zài yìqǐ jiù shì
"男孩儿"，女孩儿 和 男孩儿 在 一起 就 是

"hǎo". Wǒmen bān nǚháir, nánháir yìqǐ xué
"好"。我们 班 女孩儿、男孩儿 一起 学

Hànyǔ, hěn hǎo!
汉语，很 好！

Zhāng lǎoshī: Tóngxuémen shuō de dōu hěn yǒuyìsi. Yǐhòu nǐmen
张　老师：同学们 说 得 都 很 有意思。以后 你们

xuéxí Hànzì de shíhou duō xiǎng yì xiǎng, jiù róngyì
学习 汉字 的 时候 多 想 一 想，就 容易

jìzhù le.
记住 了。

以后 *n.*
from now on,
later

记住 *v.*
memorize

想一想 Questions

"好"字为什么是
"女"和"子"在一起，
同学们说出了哪几
种答案？

哪些汉字像"好"一样，
是两个字在一起的？
它们是什么意思？

语言点 | Language Points

一起
together, in the same place, at the same time

1. 女孩儿和男孩儿在一起就是"好"。

It is good (好) for girls (女) and boys (子) to be together.

"一起",副词,表示动作行为发生在同一地点或同一时间。

"一起" is used as an adverb to indicate that actions take place in the same place or at the same time.

(1) 你们两个站在一起,让我看看谁高一点儿。

(2) 我们两个人一起学习了四年,现在是很好的朋友。

容易
easily, likely

2. 以后你们学习汉字的时候要多想一想,就容易记住了。

From now on, think things over a little more when learning Chinese characters and you will memorize them easily.

"容易",副词,表示发生某种变化的可能性较大。

"容易" is an adverb that indicates easiness or a high degree of probability.

(1) 留学生在中国很容易学好汉语。

(2) 常常运动的人不容易生病。

练 习 | Exercises

判断正误　True (T) or false (F)

(1) "女子"是女朋友的意思。 （　　）

(2) "子"是女孩儿的意思。 （　　）

(3) 多想想汉字的意思，就容易记住汉字。 （　　）

文化略观 | Cultural Insights

会意字
Associative Compound Characters

　　会意是汉字的一种造字法，就是把两个或两个以上的独体字根据意义之间的关系合成一个字，表示两者合成的意义。有的会意字由不同的字组成，如本文中的"好"就是由"女"和"子"组成的。"武"也是个会意字，由"戈"和"止"组成，表示人拿着武器走。有的会意字由相同的字组成。如"从"，表示两人前后相随。随着语言的发展，一些会意字还沿用原来的意思，如"从"，但有的意思已有了很大改变，如"好"。

One method of Chinese character formation is the associative compound. That is to say, two or more single-component characters are combined to form a compound character with their associated meanings. Some associative compounds consist of different characters. For example, in our text "好" is formed with "女" and "子". Another example is the character "武(wǔ)", consisting of "戈(gē)" and "止(zhǐ)" with the implication of a man walking with a weapon in hand. Some associative compounds are formed with identical characters, like "从". It suggests one person follows the other. With the development of the language, people continue to use the original meanings of some associative compounds, like "从"; however, some other compounds have undergone great changes in their meaning, like "好".

4

穷和尚，富和尚
Poor Monk, Rich Monk

"做"永远比"说"好，路就在脚下！

和尚 *n.*
monk

穷 *adj.*
poor

富 *adj.*
rich

印度 *n.*
India

Cóngqián yǒu liǎng gè héshang, yí gè hěn yǒuqián, lìng yí
从前 有 两 个 和尚，一 个 很 有钱，另 一
gè hěn qióng.
个 很 穷。

　　Yǒu yì tiān, qióng héshang duì fù héshang shuō: "Wǒ xiǎng
　　有 一 天，穷 和尚 对 富 和尚 说："我 想
dào Yìndù qù xuéxí fójīng, nǐ juéde zěnmeyàng?"
到 印度 去 学习 佛经，你 觉得 怎么样？"

Fù héshang shuō: "Lù tài yuǎn le, nǐ zěnme qù ne?"
富 和尚 说："路 太 远 了，你 怎么 去 呢?"

Qióng héshang shuō: "Wǒ yǒu yí gè wǎn, yí gè bēizi hé
穷 和尚 说："我 有 一 个 碗、一 个 杯子 和

yì shuāng jiǎo, gòu le ba."
一 双 脚，够 了 吧。"

Fù héshang tīngle yǐhòu, dà xiào shuō: "Wǒ xiǎng qù Yìndù
富 和尚 听了 以后，大 笑 说："我 想 去 印度

yǐjīng yǒu hǎo duō nián le, kě yìzhí dōu méiyǒu qù, jiù shì
已经 有 好 多 年 了，可 一直 都 没有 去，就是

yīnwèi wǒ de qián bú gòu. Nǐ nàme qióng, zěnme qù de liǎo ne?"
因为 我 的 钱 不 够。你 那么 穷，怎么 去 得 了 呢?"

Sān nián yǐhòu, qióng héshang cóng Yìndù huílái le, hái
三 年 以后，穷 和尚 从 印度 回来 了，还

dàile yì běn fójīng sònggěile fù héshang. Fù héshang fēicháng
带了 一 本 佛经 送给了 富 和尚。富 和尚 非常

bùhǎoyìsi.
不好意思。

佛经 *n.*
Buddhist scripture

碗 *n.*
bowl

脚 *n.*
foot

够 *v.*
be enough, suffice

想一想 Questions

穷和尚说"一个碗、一个杯子和一双脚"就够了，为什么?

听了穷和尚的话，富和尚为什么大笑?

富和尚为什么不好意思?

语言点 Language Points

去得了
manage to go

1. 你那么穷，怎么去得了呢?
   You are so poor, how can you manage to get there?

   "去得了"是动词后接补语结构，表示做某事的可能性。"动词 + 得了"表示"能 + 动词"；"动词 + 不了"表示"不能 + 动词"。

   "去得了" is the structure of "verb + complement", which indicates the possibility of doing something. "verb + 得了" means "能 + verb", while "verb + 不了" indicates "不能 + verb".

   (1) 那儿太远了，走路去不了。
   (2) 一个西瓜 10 块钱，我有 20 块，买得了。

不好意思
feel shy / ashamed

2. 富和尚非常不好意思。
   The rich monk felt very ashamed.

   "不好意思"表示"害羞"、"惭愧"的意思。

   "不好意思" means "shy", "ashamed".

   (1) 他才考了 70 分，觉得很不好意思。
   (2) 大家都说她很漂亮，她觉得挺不好意思的。

练 习 | Exercises

判断正误　True (T) or false (F)

（1）穷和尚想让富和尚跟他一起去印度。　　　　　（　　）

（2）富和尚没想过去印度。　　　　　　　　　　　（　　）

（3）富和尚觉得钱不够不可能去印度。　　　　　　（　　）

（4）穷和尚最后成功（chénggōng：successful）地去了印度。　（　　）

文化略观 | Cultural Insights

佛教在中国
Buddhism in China

佛教是与基督教、伊斯兰教并列的世界三大宗教之一。公元前六世纪至公元前五世纪，佛教由释迦牟尼创建于古印度，并开始向境外传播。据记载，西汉时期佛教传入中国。在漫长的历史过程中，佛教在中国已远远超出了宗教范围，逐渐渗透到中国文化的各个领域，包括语言文字、哲学思想、史学艺术、科技建筑、乃至民风民俗，成为中国传统文化的重要组成部分。

乐山大佛（Lèshān Dàfó）
Giant Stone Buddha in Leshan City, Sichuan Province

Along with Christianity and Islam, Buddhism is one of the three most influential religions in the world. It was established by Sakyamuni in ancient India between the 6th and 5th century BC, and then began to spread abroad. It is recorded that Buddhism was introduced into China in the time of the Western Han Dynasty. Over the course of its long history, Buddhism has become much more than a religious belief in China, and has gradually penetrated all aspects of Chinese culture, including language, philosophy, history, the arts, science, architecture, and even folk customs. Consequently, it has become an important part of traditional Chinese culture.

5

议价
Bargaining

你在中国砍过价吗？
如果你会砍价，就能买到便宜的东西。

议价/砍价 *v.*
bargain

对话 *n.*
dialogue

zài Zhōngguó mǎi dōngxi hěn tèbié, nà jiù shì kěyǐ kǎnjià.
在 中国 买 东西 很 特别，那 就 是 可以 砍价。
Xiàmian shì wǒ zuótiān mǎi dōngxi kǎnjià de duìhuà.
下面 是 我 昨天 买 东西 砍价 的 对话。

Lǎobǎn: Zhè jiàn yīfu hěn piàoliang, shìshi ba!
老板：这 件 衣服 很 漂亮，试试 吧!

Wǒ : Duōshao qián?
我 ： 多少 钱?

Lǎobǎn: Bú guì, 160 kuài.
老板：不 贵，160 块。

Wǒ : Á? Tài guì le!

我 : 啊？太 贵 了！

Lǎobǎn: Nǐ shuō duōshao qián?

老板 : 你 说 多少 钱？

Wǒ : 100 kuài.

我 : 100 块 。

Lǎobǎn: Á? Tài shǎo le, bú mài.

老板 : 啊？太 少 了，不 卖 。

Wǒ : Nà wǒ zǒu le.

我 : 那 我 走 了。

Lǎobǎn: Ài, děngdeng, 130 zěnmeyàng?

老板 : 唉， 等等， 130 怎么样？

Wǒ : 130 tài guì le, wǒ shì xuésheng, méiyǒu qián.

我 : 130 太 贵 了，我 是 学生， 没有 钱。

Lǎobǎn: Zuì duō duōshao qián?

老板 : 最 多 多少 钱？

Wǒ : 100 kuài.

我 : 100 块 。

Lǎobǎn: OK le, dōu tuì yí bù, 120 kuài zěnmeyàng?

老板 : OK 了，都 退 一 步，120 块 怎么样？

Wǒ : Hǎo ba.

我 : 好 吧。

Lǎobǎn: Gěi nǐ yīfu. Huānyíng xià cì zài lái!

老板 : 给 你 衣服。 欢迎 下 次 再 来！

等等
wait a minute

退一步
to make a
compromise

退 v.
retreat

步 n.
step

想一想 Questions

在你的国家，买东西
可以砍价吗？

你喜欢砍价吗？

语言点 Language Points

试试
have a try

1. 这件衣服很漂亮，试试吧！

This item of clothing looks very good. Try it on!

"试"，动词，表示为了看到效果而做某事，尝试。"试试"表示动作持续时间短，可以单独用或在后面加上"试"的对象。

"试" is a verb that means to test or try. "试试" indicates that an action lasts for a short period of time. It can be used alone or with an object after it.

（1）小姐，我能试试这双鞋吗？

（2）我刚买了一个手机，你试试吧。

太
too much

2. 太贵了！

Too expensive!

"太 + 形容词 / 动词"中的"太"是副词，表示程度高，句末常带"了"。

In the structure "太 + adjective / verb", "太" is an adverb that indicates too much, and is often used with "了" at the end of the sentence.

（1）最近我太忙，没时间去你那儿了。

（2）穷和尚太穷了，他只有一个碗和一个杯子。

练 习 | **Exercises**

选择正确答案　Choose the correct answer.

(1) 在中国买东西很特别，是因为（　　）。

　　A. 中国东西便宜　　B. 在中国可以砍价　　C. 中国东西很贵

(2) 砍价时所用的话语不包括（　　）。

　　A. 太贵了　　　　　B. 我走了　　　　　　C. 买东西

(3) 最后"我"用（　　）钱买到了那件衣服。

　　A. 100 块　　　　　B. 120 块　　　　　　C. 130 块

文化略观 | **Cultural Insights**

在哪些地方可以砍价？
Where is it OK to Bargain?

　　中国人买东西有砍价的习惯，但不是所有地方都可以砍价。一般来说，大街上的小货摊可以砍价，但是价钱不会便宜很多。不过，在一些小商品市场里，往往可以用要价的 50% 甚至更低的价钱买到商品。但在大型购物中心，如果没有打折降价的标志，一般都明码标价。在这种商场中，如果砍价，会被认为不礼貌，或并不是真心想买东西。

The Chinese like to bargain when shopping, but prices cannot be haggled over everywhere. Generally speaking, you can bargain at stalls in the street, but not by a lot. In some small markets, you can pay half the price offered or even lower. In big shopping malls, however, prices are clearly marked, unless they have discount labels. In this kind of shopping centre, it is generally considered impolite, or that you are not really interested in buying, if you try bargaining.

6

自行车王国
Bicycle Kingdom

在中国，骑自行车的人特别多，
所以中国是个"自行车王国"。

骑 v.
ride

大街 n.
avenue

潮水 n.
tide

Yīnwèi qí zìxíngchē de rén fēicháng duō, suǒyǐ yǒu rén shuō
因为 骑 自行车 的 人 非常 多，所以 有 人 说
Zhōngguó shì "zìxíngchē wángguó".
中国 是 "自行车 王国 "。
Zài Zhōngguó de chéngshì li, rúguǒ shì shàng-xiàbān shíjiān,
在 中国 的 城市 里，如果 是 上下班 时间，
dàjiē shang de zìxíngchē jiù xiàng cháoshuǐ yíyàng. Mǎi yí liàng
大街 上 的 自行车 就 像 潮水 一样。买 一 辆

zìxíngchē zhǐ yào jǐ bǎi yuán, hěn piányi, yīncǐ hěn duō Zhōngguó
自行车 只 要 几 百 元，很 便宜，因此 很 多 中国

jiātíng měi rén dōu yǒu yí liàng zìxíngchē. Zhōngguó de yìxiē
家庭 每 人 都 有 一 辆 自行车。 中国 的 一些

dàxué xiàoyuán hěn dà, hěn duō dàxuéshēng yě yǒu zìxíngchē.
大学 校园 很 大，很 多 大学生 也 有 自行车。

　　Zài Měiguó hé Ōuzhōu, rénmen qí zìxíngchē chángcháng shì
　　在 美国 和 欧洲，人们 骑 自行车 常常 是

wèile duànliàn shēntǐ. Ér zài Zhōngguó, zìxíngchē zhǔyào shì jiāotōng
为了 锻炼 身体。而 在 中国， 自行车 主要 是 交通

gōngjù. Zìxíngchē fēicháng huánbǎo, yǒu hěn duō yōudiǎn. Kěshì,
工具。 自行车 非常 环保，有 很 多 优点。可是，

jìnniánlái, Zhōngguó de xiǎoqìchē yuèláiyuè duō, dà chéngshì de
近年来， 中国 的 小汽车 越来越 多，大 城市 的

dǔchē yě yuèláiyuè yánzhòng. Zhēn xīwàng Zhōngguó jìxù zuò yí
堵车 也 越来越 严重。 真 希望 中国 继续 做 一

gè "zìxíngchē wángguó".
个 "自行车 王国 "。

锻炼 v.	exercise
交通 n.	transportation
工具 n.	vehicle
环保 n.	environmental protection
优点 n.	merit, advantage
堵车 n.	traffic jam
严重 adj.	severe, serious
继续 v.	continue

想一想 Questions

你觉得自行车有什么优点?

欧美人骑自行车主要是为了什么?

作者为什么希望中国继续做一个 "自行车王国"?

语言点 Language Points

因此
therefore, so

1. ……很便宜，因此很多中国家庭每人都有一辆自行车。

   (It is) very cheap, so in many Chinese families, each person has a bike.

   "因此"用来说明结果。

   " 因此 " is used to introduce results.

   （1）我喜欢中国，因此来北京学习汉语。

   （2）我昨天睡得太晚了，因此今天上课迟到了。

越来越
more and more

2. 近年来，中国的小汽车越来越多，大城市的堵车也越来越严重。

   In recent years, there have been more and more cars in China, and the traffic jams in big cities have got more and more severe.

   "越来越"表示程度随时间的推移而升级。

   " 越来越 " means a rise in degree as time goes on.

   （1）到了五月，南京的天气就越来越热了。

   （2）事情越来越有希望，咱们再等一等吧。

练 习 Exercises

判断正误　True (T) or false (F)

（1）中国是"自行车王国"，因为中国的自行车最好。　　（　　）

（2）在中国，现在买一辆自行车不会花很多钱。　　（　　）

（3）欧洲人、美国人骑自行车的原因和中国人不一样。　　（　　）

（4）"我"觉得中国应该有更多的小汽车。　　（　　）

文 化 略 观 Cultural Insights

自行车在中国
Bicycles in China

　　以前，自行车在中国的家庭中曾经占据重要地位。它与手表、缝纫机一起被称为"三大件"，是中国家庭财富的象征。改革开放（1978 年）以后，人们的生活水平提高了，特别是近些年，私家车已经在一定程度上取代了自行车，成为许多城市居民的代步工具。但越来越多的机动车给交通和环境带来了不良影响，因此，自行车在一定时期内仍将是政府提倡和人们喜爱的交通工具。

Bicycles used to play an important role in Chinese families. They were one of the "Three Important Items" together with watches and sewing machines, which were regarded as symbols of family wealth. Since the "reform and opening up" of 1978, people's living standards have improved. In recent years in particular, cars have taken the place of bicycles to a certain degree, and are becoming the main form of transport for people living in cities. But having more and more cars has caused traffic and environmental problems. Because of this, for now bicycles will still be promoted by the government and remain popular among the Chinese people.

7 | 看风景还是拍照片？
Sightseeing or Photographing?

旅行的时候，有的人喜欢看风景（fēngjǐng：scenery），
有的人喜欢拍照片。你在旅行的时候喜欢拍照片吗？

欣赏 *v.*
appreciate

架 *m.*
(used for sth.
with a stand or
mechanism)

Yǒu yì zhāng hěn yǒuqù de huà, gàosu dàjiā Zhōngguórén
有 一 张 很 有趣 的 画，告诉 大家 中国人
hé Xīfāngrén zài lǚyóu shí de biǎoxiàn shì bùtóng de. Yòubian de
和 西方人 在 旅游 时 的 表现 是 不同 的。右边 的
huà li yǒu yì zhī yǎnjing, dàibiǎo Xīfāngrén, yìsi shì Xīfāngrén
画 里 有 一 只 眼睛，代表 西方人，意思 是 西方人
lǚyóu de shíhou, xǐhuan yòng zìjǐ de yǎnjing xīnshǎng měijǐng.
旅游 的 时候，喜欢 用 自己 的 眼睛 欣赏 美景。
Zuǒbian de huà li shì yí jià xiàngjī, dàibiǎo Zhōngguórén, yìsi
左边 的 画 里 是 一 架 相机，代表 中国人， 意思

shì Zhōngguórén lǚyóu de shíhou, xǐhuan dàizhe xiàngjī dàochù
是 中国人 旅游 的 时候，喜欢 带着 相机 到处
pāizhào.
拍照。

　　Quèshí, yǐqián Zhōngguórén lǚyóu de jīhuì hěn shǎo, chūguó
　　确实，以前 中国人 旅游 的 机会 很 少，出国
lǚyóu de jīhuì gèng shǎo, suǒyǐ, hěn duō rén dōu xǐhuan yòng
旅游 的 机会 更 少，所以，很 多 人 都 喜欢 用
xiàngjī dàitì yǎnjing. Tāmen bùtíng de pāizhào, huídào jiā yǐhòu,
相机 代替 眼睛。他们 不停 地 拍照，回到 家 以后，
yìbiān kàn zhàopiàn, yìbiān huíyì qùguo de dìfang. Suízhe Zhōngguó
一边 看 照片，一边 回忆 去过 的 地方。随着 中国
jīngjì de fāzhǎn, yuèláiyuè duō de Zhōngguórén chūqù lǚyóu,
经济 的 发展，越来越 多 的 中国人 出去 旅游，
rénmen yě yuèláiyuè yìshí dào, kànzhe zhàopiàn huíyì suīrán
人们 也 越来越 意识 到，看着 照片 回忆 虽然
zhòngyào, dàn gèng zhòngyào de háishi yòng zìjǐ de yǎnjing
重要，但 更 重要 的 还是 用 自己 的 眼睛
xīnshǎng yǎnqián de měijǐng.
欣赏 眼前 的 美景。

拍照 *v.*
take photos

确实 *adv.*
indeed

机会 *n.*
chance

意识 *v.*
realize

想一想 Questions

你觉得旅行时
相机很重要吗？
为什么？

西方人和中国人的旅行
方式，你喜欢哪一种？
为什么？

语言点 Language Points

代表
represent,
stand for

1. 右边的画里有一只眼睛，代表西方人。
There is an eye on the right of the picture, representing westerners.

　　"代表"，动词，表示用人或事物表示某种特定的意义或概念。"代表"前面的内容是客观的、可以被感知的事物，后面的内容通常是这种事物被赋予的某种意义。

　　"代表" is a verb that means certain people or things can serve as a sign or symbol (of somebody or something). The part before "代表" is usually an objective thing that can be perceived, while the part after "代表" is the meaning represented by the previous part.

　　（1）中国人喜欢数字"8"，因为"8"代表"发"（有很多钱）。
　　（2）在有的国家，点头代表不同意，摇头代表同意。

代替
substitute,
instead of

2. 很多人都喜欢用相机代替眼睛。
Many people liked to use their cameras instead of their eyes.

　　"A 代替 B"中，"代替"是动词，这一句式表示用 A 换 B，由 A 起 B 的作用。

　　"代替" in "A代替B" is a verb. This pattern means to substitute B with A; A plays the role of B.

　　（1）今天王老师生病了，张老师代替他给我们上课。
　　（2）比赛就要开始了，小明还没来，我们找谁来代替他呢？

随着
along with

3. 随着中国经济的发展，越来越多的中国人出去旅游。
With China's economic development, more and more Chinese people are beginning to travel abroad.

　　"随着"，动词，表示某事与另一件事一起发生的意思。
　　"随着" is a verb that means something happens along with something else.

　　（1）随着我的汉语水平的提高，我越来越喜欢北京的生活了。
　　（2）随着春天的到来，公园里更加热闹了。

练习 Exercises

判断正误 True (T) or false (F)

（1）以前中国人旅游的机会不多。　　　　　　　　（　　）

（2）中国人出去旅游很喜欢拍照。　　　　　　　　（　　）

（3）西方人旅游更喜欢用眼睛去欣赏美景。　　　　（　　）

（4）越来越多的中国人出去旅行，因为他们有钱了。（　　）

文化略观 Cultural Insights

旅游
Tourism

　　随着人们收入的提高，旅游已日渐成为中国人的时尚生活方式。中国旅游资源丰富，传统的旅游地区有北京、西安等历史名城。近年来，新疆、西藏、云南等西部少数民族聚居区也受到越来越多国内外游客的青睐。同时，出国游不再是奢侈行为，很多人把东南亚、欧洲等地区作为出行的目的地。

With people's income increasing, tourism is becoming a popular part of Chinese people's lifestyle. China is rich in tourism opportunities. Traditional places of interest include historical cities like Beijing and Xi'an. In recent years, the home areas of ethnic groups in the western parts of China, like Xinjiang, Tibet and Yunnan, have attracted more and more travellers from home and abroad. At the same time, travelling abroad is no longer a luxury. Many people choose regions like South-East Asia and Europe as their travel destinations.

8

傻 酒 鬼
Funny Drunks

你爱喝酒吗？

喝酒以后闹过笑话吗？

酒鬼 *n.*
drunk

外面 *n.*
outside

公寓 *n.*
apartment building

Yǒu fù-zǐ liǎng rén, dōu shì jiǔguǐ, tāmen tèbié ài hējiǔ,
有 父子 两 人，都 是 酒鬼，他们 特别 爱 喝酒，

yě jīngcháng hēzuì.
也 经常 喝醉。

Yì tiān, fùqīn zài wàimian hē de dà zuì, yáoyáohuànghuàng
一 天，父亲 在 外面 喝 得 大 醉， 摇摇晃晃

huídào tāmen zhù de gōngyù. Tāmen jiā zhù zài sān lóu, kěshì
回到 他们 住 的 公寓。 他们 家 住 在 三 楼，可是

32

tā zài èr lóu jiù qiāo mén le.　Èr lóu de rén méi kāi mén jiù shuō:
他 在 二 楼 就 敲 门 了。二 楼 的 人 没 开 门 就 说:

"Nǐmen jiā zài lóu shàng!" Fùqīn hǎobù róngyì huídào jiā, jìnmén
"你们 家 在 楼 上!" 父亲 好不 容易 回到 家, 进门

hòu, tā dīngzhe érzi de liǎn kànle yíhuìr, shēngqì de shuō: "Qíguài,
后, 他 盯着 儿子 的 脸 看了 一会儿, 生气 地 说:"奇怪,

nǐ de liǎn zěnme biànchéng sān gè le? Nǐ zhèyàng yí gè qíguài
你 的 脸 怎么 变成 三 个 了? 你 这样 一 个 奇怪

de dōngxi, wǒ de fángzi yídìng bù liúgěi nǐ!" Tā de érzi yě zài
的 东西, 我 的 房子 一定 不 留给 你!" 他 的 儿子 也 在

jiā hē de dà zuì, tīngle bàba de huà, bù fúqì de shuō: "Nà
家 喝 得 大 醉, 听了 爸爸 的 话, 不 服气 地 说:"那

gèng hǎo! Xiàng zhèyàng yáoyáohuànghuàng de fángzi, gěi wǒ, wǒ
更 好! 像 这样 摇摇晃晃 的 房子, 给 我, 我

hái bú yào ne!"
还 不 要 呢!"

敲 *v.*	knock
盯 *v.*	stare at
生气 *v.*	get angry
留 *v.*	leave behind
服气 *adj.*	convinced

想一想 Questions

儿子觉得父亲的房子
好不好? 为什么?

父亲为什么
摇摇晃晃地回家?

?

语言点 Language Points

喝得大醉
very drunk

1. 一天，父亲在外面喝得大醉。
One day, the father went out and got very drunk.

"喝得大醉"是"动词＋得＋形容词"的结构，其中形容词作动词的补语，表示动作或动作发出者的状态。

The structure of "喝得大醉" is "verb＋得＋adjective". The adjective is used as a complement of the verb and indicates the state of the action or the person who does the action.

（1）她中国菜做得非常好。
（2）他的汉语说得真棒!

摇摇晃晃
stumbling

2.（父亲）摇摇晃晃回到他们住的公寓。
(The father) stumbled back to the apartment building where they lived.

"摇摇晃晃"，是动词"摇晃"的重叠形式，表示摇摆晃动的样子。

"摇摇晃晃" is a reduplication pattern of the verb "摇晃" and indicates the state of stumbling.

（1）这个人不喜欢工作，每天吃吃喝喝，什么也不做。
（2）生日晚会的时候，大家在一起说说笑笑，很热闹。

练 习 | Exercises

选择正确答案　Choose the correct answer.

（1）父亲和儿子都喜欢（　　）。

    A. 买东西　　　　　　B. 吸烟　　　　　　C. 喝酒

（2）他们家住在（　　）。

    A. 一楼　　　　　　　B. 二楼　　　　　　C. 三楼

（3）因为（　　），所以二楼的人没有开门。

    A. 父亲经常敲错门　　B. 他们在休息　　　C. 他们在喝酒

文化略观 | **Cultural Insights**

中国的"酒文化"
Chinese "Alcohol Culture"

酒在中国有着独特的地位，影响着中国人生活的很多方面。从文学、饮食、保健到人际交往，从国宴到普通人的聚餐，到处都能看到酒的身影。古诗中也有无数关于酒的名句，因为中国古代文人诗必饮酒，酒必赋诗。像右图中的陶渊明和左图中的李白都在酒后留下了许多伟大的诗篇。

Alcohol occupies a unique role in China. It influences many aspects of Chinese people's lives. From literature, diet and health care to social communication, from state banquets to ordinary gatherings of common people, the influence of drinking can be seen everywhere. There are also numerous famous lines about drink in classic Chinese poems, because in ancient times, Chinese men of letters always drank when they wrote poetry, just as shown in the pictures of Tao Yuanming (right) and Li Bai (left), two great poets who created many masterpieces after a few drinks.

9

磨斧子
Whet the Axe

在人的一生（yīshēng: all one's life）中，
我们应该经常停下来想一想，这样才能走得更快、更好。

难道是我的力气越来越小了？

斧子 n.
axe

伐木工人 n.
lumberjack

条件 n.
condition

砍 v.
chop, cut down

Yǒu gè niánqīng de fámù gōngrén, hǎobù róngyì zhǎodàole
有 个 年轻 的 伐木 工人 ， 好不 容易 找到了
yí fèn gōngzuò, gōngzuò tiáojiàn hěn hǎo. Tā hěn xǐhuan zhè fèn
一 份 工作， 工作 条件 很 好。他 很 喜欢 这 份
gōngzuò, xià juéxīn hǎohǎo gàn.
工作， 下 决心 好好 干。

　　Dì-yī tiān, tā kǎnle 18 kē shù. Lǎobǎn hěn gāoxìng de
　　第一 天，他 砍了 18 棵 树。老板 很 高兴 地
gǔlì tā: "Bú cuò!" Niánqīng de gōngrén hěn gāoxìng.
鼓励 他："不 错！" 年轻 的 工人 很 高兴。

Dì-èr tiān, tā yìzhí gōngzuò, dànshì zhǐ kǎnle 15 kē shù.
第二 天，他 一直 工作， 但是 只 砍了 15 棵 树。

Dì-sān tiān, tā háishi fēicháng nǔlì, kěshì zhǐ kǎnle 10 kē shù.
第三 天，他 还是 非常 努力，可是 只 砍了 10 棵 树。

Gōngrén gǎndào hěn cánkuì, dào lǎobǎn nàli dàoqiàn shuō: "Bù
工人 感到 很 惭愧，到 老板 那里 道歉 说："不

zhīdào wèishénme, wǒ yǐjīng hěn nǔlì le, dànshì wǒ de lìqi què
知道 为什么，我 已经 很 努力 了，但是 我 的 力气 却

yuèláiyuè xiǎo."
越来越 小 。"

Lǎobǎn wèn tā: "Nǐ shàng yí cì mó fǔzi shì zài shénme
老板 问 他："你 上 一 次 磨 斧子 是 在 什么

shíhou?"
时候？"

"Mó fǔzi?" Gōngrén tūrán míngbai le, "Wǒ tiāntiān mángzhe
"磨 斧子？" 工人 突然 明白 了，"我 天天 忙着

kǎn shù, dàn wàngle mó fǔzi le!"
砍 树，但 忘了 磨 斧子 了！"

惭愧 *adj.*	ashamed
道歉 *v.*	apologize
力气 *n.*	strength
磨 *v.*	sharpen
明白 *v.*	understand, realize
忙 *v.*	be busy

想一想 **Questions**

为什么工人
砍的树越来越少？

这个故事告诉
我们什么？

语言点 Language Points

下决心
make up
one's mind,
be determined

1. 他很喜欢这份工作，下决心好好干。

He liked his job very much, and was determined to do it well.

"下决心"，表示拿定主意，有决心干某事。"决心"，名词，表示坚定的意志。

"下决心" indicates to be determined to do something. "决心" is a noun that means "strong will".

（1）我常常因为声调闹笑话，所以我下决心学好汉语的发音。
（2）北京的房子很贵，所以许多人下决心不买房子了。

鼓励
inspire, encourage

2. 老板很高兴地鼓励他："不错！"

The boss was very happy and encouraged him: "Well done!"

"鼓励"，动词，是"激发、勉励"的意思。

"鼓励" is a verb that means "to inspire and encourage".

（1）老师常常鼓励我们，我们的学习也更努力了。
（2）非常感谢你对我的鼓励，我一定好好干！

练 习 | Exercises

选择正确答案　Choose the correct answer.

(1) 伐木工人很喜欢这份工作，不是因为（　　　）。

　　A. 工作条件很好　　B. 找工作不容易　　C. 这份工作很容易

(2) 从第一天到第三天，工人砍的树（　　　）。

　　A. 越来越多　　　　B. 越来越少　　　　C. 每天都一样

(3) 第三天，工人感到（　　　）。

　　A. 很高兴　　　　　B. 很伤心　　　　　C. 很不好意思

(4) 工人砍树越来越少的原因是（　　　）。

　　A. 他工作不努力　　B. 他没有磨斧子　　C. 他的力气越来越小

文化略观 | Cultural Insights

磨刀不误砍柴工
Whetting the Axe Will Not
Delay the Cutting of Firewood

　　中国有句老话，叫"磨刀不误砍柴工"。意思是说，花点时间把斧子磨得锋利些，就可以提高砍柴的效率，不会耽误砍柴的时间。这句话强调花时间做好准备工作，不会耽误工作进度，而且往往能取得"事半功倍"的效果。

　　There is an old Chinese saying, "Whetting the axe will not delay the cutting of firewood". This saying means that spending some time sharpening the axe will let you chop wood with more efficiency, and won't cost you time. It implies that good preparation saves time, just as "a stitch in time saves nine".

10 北京的出租车
Taxis in Beijing

来过北京的人都说，
北京的出租车司机真热情。

起步价 *n.*
starting price

之后 *n.*
from then on

大概 *adv.*
approximately

Zài Běijīng chéng chūzūchē hěn fāngbiàn. Qǐbùjià shì sān
在 北京 乘 出租车 很 方便。起步价 是 三
qiānmǐ shí kuài qián, zhīhòu yì qiānmǐ liǎng kuài qián. Bǐrú, cóng
千米 十 块 钱，之后 一 千米 两 块 钱。比如，从
jīchǎng dào Běijīng Dàxué sìshí duō qiānmǐ, dàgài yìbǎi kuài qián.
机场 到 北京 大学 四十 多 千米，大概 一百 块 钱。

Běijīngrén yìbān bǎ chūzūchē jiàozuò "dīshì" huòzhě "chūzū",
北京人 一般 把 出租车 叫做 "的士" 或者 "出租"，

zuò chūzūchē jiào "dǎdī", "dǎchē". Běijīng de chūzūchē sījī
坐 出租车 叫"打的"、"打车"。北京 的 出租车 司机

bèi qīnqiè de chēngwéi "dīgē", "dījiě". Dàn "dīgē", "dījiě"
被 亲切 地 称为 "的哥"、"的姐"。但 "的哥"、"的姐"

hěn shǎo dāngmiàn yòng, dāngmiàn yìbān shuō "shīfu". Běijīng de
很 少 当面 用, 当面 一般 说 "师傅"。北京 的

chūzūchē sījī hěn yǒuyìsi, tāmen xǐhuan hé nǐ liáotiānr, nǐ
出租车 司机 很 有意思, 他们 喜欢 和 你 聊天儿, 你

yǒu shénme bù zhīdào de, dōu kéyǐ wèn tāmen. Tāmen fēicháng
有 什么 不 知道 的, 都 可以 问 他们。他们 非常

rèqíng, yuànyì huídá gèzhǒng-gèyàng de wèntí.
热情, 愿意 回答 各种各样 的 问题。

　　Lìngwài, zuò chūzūchē de shíhou yào jìzhù: dì-yī, bié wàngle
　　另外, 坐 出租车 的 时候 要 记住:第一,别 忘了

nǐ de dōngxi; dì-èr, cóng yòubian chēmén shàng-xiàchē.
你 的 东西;第二,从 右边 车门 上下车。

亲切 *adj.*
affectionate

当面 *adv.*
face to face

愿意 *adj.*
willing

各种各样
all kinds of

另外 *conj.*
in addition

想一想 Questions

语言点 Language Points

从……到……
from … to …

1. 从机场到北京大学四十多千米，大概一百块钱。

It is more than 40 kilometres from the airport to Peking University and costs approximately 100 *yuan*.

"从……到……"，意思是由一点到另一点，表示范围、距离、状态或时间的变化。

"从……到……" means "from … to …", and is used to show changes in scope, distance, condition or time.

（1）从北京到东京，坐飞机大概要三个小时。

（2）我每天从早上八点到中午十二点有课。

别
not to do

2. 别忘了你的东西。

Do not forget your belongings.

"别"，副词，表示建议某人不要做某事。

"别" is an adverb that advises somebody not to do something.

（1）现在都八点半了，以后早点儿来，别迟到。

（2）下雨了，今天别出去了。

练 习 | Exercises

判断正误　True (T) or false (F)

（1）北京出租车起步价是十千米三块钱。　　　（　　）

（2）出租车三千米以后每千米两块钱。　　　　（　　）

（3）北京的出租车司机喜欢和客人聊天儿。　　（　　）

（4）你可以问出租车司机各种各样的问题。　　（　　）

文化略观 | Cultural Insights

黄包车的今昔
Rickshaws Today and Yesterday

　　黄包车是一种用人力拖拉的双轮客运工具，它的英文名来自"人力车"的日语读音——jinrikisha，意思是"人力拖动的车"。黄包车在 1874 年从日本输入上海，上海政府下令所有的出租人力车都要漆成黄色，"黄包车"因此而得名。后来黄包车在中国各大城市纷纷使用。一直到 20 世纪 50 年代被送进博物馆，黄包车才一度退出了历史舞台。但近年来，在北京的"胡同游"和杭州的"西湖游"等旅游活动中，黄包车又恢复了往日的生机。

The rickshaw is a small, two-wheeled, man-powered passenger vehicle. The English name comes from the Japanese reading of "人力车"— *jinrikisha* — meaning "man-powered vehicle". It was introduced to Shanghai from Japan in 1874. The Shanghai government ordered all public-hire rickshaws be painted yellow, and so the Chinese name came to be "黄包车". It was widely used in big cities in China until the 1950s, when it was consigned to the museum. However, in recent years, it has been revived as a tourist attraction, such as in Beijing's "Hutong Tour" and Hangzhou's "West Lake Sightseeing Tour".

11

黑猩猩戒烟
The Chimp that Quit Smoking

你吸烟吗？有没有戒过烟？成功了吗？
下面是一个黑猩猩吸烟、戒烟的有趣故事。

动物园 *n.*
zoo

黑猩猩 *n.*
chimpanzee

扔 *v.*
throw

Fēifēi shì dòngwùyuán de yì zhī hēixīngxing, tā fēicháng
非非是 动物园 的 一 只 黑猩猩，它 非常
kě'ài. Kěshì, lái dòngwùyuán wánr de rén chángcháng xiàng tā
可爱。可是，来 动物园 玩儿 的 人 常常 向 它
rēng yāntóu. Mànmàn de, Fēifēi yě kāishǐ xīyān. Tā yuè xī yuè duō,
扔 烟头。慢慢 地,非非 也 开始 吸烟。它 越 吸 越 多,

yǒushí yì tiān yào xī shí zhī yān.
有时 一 天 要 吸 十 支 烟。

    Yīnwèi xīyān tài duō, Fēifēi de shēntǐ yuèláiyuè chà. Zài
因为 吸烟 太 多，非非 的 身体 越来越 差。在

chūntiān, Fēifēi gǎnmàole hǎo jǐ cì, érqiě hái déle fèiyán.
春天， 非非 感冒了 好 几 次，而且 还 得了 肺炎。

    Dòngwùyuán de gōngzuò rényuán dǎsuan ràng Fēifēi jiè yān.
动物园 的 工作 人员 打算 让 非非 戒 烟。

Kāishǐ shí, gōngzuò rényuán yì tiān gěi tā shí zhī, hòulái bā zhī,
开始 时， 工作 人员 一 天 给 它 十 支，后来 八 支、

wǔ zhī, yuèláiyuè shǎo. Fēifēi xiǎng xīyān shí, gōngzuò rényuán jiù
五 支，越来越 少。 非非 想 吸烟 时，工作 人员 就

gěi tā hē niúnǎi. Tóngshí gōngzuò rényuán hái gàosu dàjiā, búyào
给 它 喝 牛奶。 同时 工作 人员 还 告诉 大家，不要

zài gěi Fēifēi yān le.
再 给 非非 烟 了。

    Liǎng gè yuè yǐhòu, Fēifēi chénggōng de jièle yān.
两 个 月 以后，非非 成功 地 戒了 烟。

烟头 *n.*	cigarette butt
吸烟 *v.*	smoke
感冒 *v.*	catch a cold
肺炎 *n.*	pneumonia
人员 *n.*	personnel, staff
戒烟 *v.*	quit smoking
成功 *adv.*	successfully

想一想 Questions

非非是怎么开始吸烟的?

非非又是怎么戒烟的?

语言点 Language Points

得
get

1. 在春天，非非感冒了好几次，而且还得了肺炎。

   In spring, Feifei caught a cold several times, and even got pneumonia.

   "得"，动词，是"得到"的意思，和"失"相对。

   "得" is a verb that means "get", the opposite of "lose".

   (1) 这次考试你得了多少分？
   (2) 经常不吃早饭，容易得病。

打算
plan, consider

2. 动物园的工作人员打算让非非戒烟。

   The staff of the zoo made a plan to make Feifei quit smoking.

   "打算"，动词，是"考虑、计划"的意思。

   "打算" is a verb that means to think about something and make plans.

   (1) 这个星期天，我打算去爬长城。
   (2) 你打算什么时候走？

练 习 Exercises

判断正误　True (T) or false (F)

（1）是动物园的工作人员让非非学习吸烟的。　　（　　）

（2）因为吸烟，所以非非得了肺炎。　　（　　）

（3）非非很容易就戒烟了。　　（　　）

（4）最后非非不吸烟了。　　（　　）

文化略观 Cultural Insights

中国的烟民和禁烟政策
China's Smokers and No-Smoking Policies

　　以前，中国的烟民很多，人们对吸烟也没有太多限制。在公共场所，不吸烟的人不得不吸"二手烟"。但现在，中国的室内公共场所大多禁止吸烟，法律还规定不得向未成年人售烟，烟草不得进行广告宣传。人们也逐渐意识到吸烟对身体的危害。

There used to be lots of smokers in China, and smoking was not restricted in public places. Those who did not smoke became victims of "second-hand smoke" against their will. However, nowadays in China, smoking is forbidden in most public indoor places. Laws have been made against selling cigarettes to teenagers, and cigarettes cannot be advertised. People have gradually become aware of the harm smoking does to health.

12

量词与名词
Measure Words and Nouns

每个语言都有名词，可是很多语言没有量词。
汉语有很多量词，而且汉语的量词和名词还是一对好朋友。

一双　　一副　　一对

量词 *n.*
measure word

前面 *n.*
front

离不开 *adj.*
inseparable

厨房 *n.*
kitchen

Hànyǔ de liàngcí chángcháng zài míngcí de qiánmian, liàngcí
汉语 的 量词 常常 在 名词 的 前面，量词

líbukāi míngcí, míngcí yě líbukāi liàngcí. Dàjiā kànkan wǒ yì tiān
离不开 名词，名词 也 离不开 量词。大家 看看 我 一 天

de shēnghuó jiù zhīdào le.
的 生活 就 知道 了。

Wǒ zǎoshang 7:30 qǐchuáng, xiān qù chúfáng, hēle yì píng
我 早上 7:30 起床，先 去 厨房，喝了 一 瓶

niúnǎi, chī le sān piàn miànbāo hé yí gè píngguǒ,ránhòu huídào
牛奶，吃了 三 片 面包 和 一 个 苹果，然后 回到

fángjiān li, chuānshàng yí jiàn yīfu, yì shuāng xié, bēiqǐ yí
房间 里， 穿上 一 件 衣服、 一 双 鞋，背起 一

gè shūbāo (shūbāo li yǒu sān běn shū, liǎng zhī bǐ hé yí gè
个 书包 （书包 里 有 三 本 书、 两 支 笔 和 一 个

shǒujī) qù xuéxiào.
手机） 去 学校。

Zài lùshang, wǒ kàndào yì zhī kě'ài de xiǎo gǒu.
在 路上， 我 看到 一 只 可爱 的 小 狗。

Dàole jiàoshì, wǒ kànjiàn qiáng shang xīn tiēle yì zhāng Zhōngguó
到了 教室，我 看见 墙 上 新 贴了 一 张 中国

dìtú. Kuài shàngkè le, jìnlái yí wèi lǎoshī, tā dàizhe yí fù
地图。 快 上课 了，进来 一 位 老师，他 戴着 一 副

yǎnjìng. Sì jié kè yǐhòu wǒmen qù shítáng chīfàn, wǒ yàole yì
眼镜。四 节 课 以后 我们 去 食堂 吃饭，我 要了 一

píng píjiǔ, hái yǒu yí fèn Xīhóngshì Chǎo Jīdàn.
瓶 啤酒，还 有 一 份 西红柿 炒 鸡蛋。

背 v.
carry (on the back)

地图 n.
map

戴 v.
wear

炒 v.
stir-fry

想一想 Questions

"我"的书包里
有什么?

教室里有什么?

"我"中午
吃了什么?

语言点 Language Points

先……然后……
first …, then …

1. 我……先去厨房……然后回到房间里……

First I went into the kitchen, and then went back to the bedroom.

"先……然后……"表示一件事情之后接着又发生另一件事情。

"先……然后……" indicates an event takes place immediately after another event.

（1）下车时，先给司机钱，然后说"谢谢"。
（2）我学汉语的时候，先学拼音，然后学汉字。

快
soon, before long

2. 快上课了，进来一位老师。

When the class was about to begin, a teacher came in.

"快"，副词，表示将要出现某种情况。

"快" is an adverb that indicates something will happen a short time from now.

（1）妈妈说："赶紧起床！快迟到了！"
（2）天快亮的时候，下雨了。

副
(a) pair of

3. 他戴着一副眼镜。

He wore a pair of glasses.

"副"，量词，用于成套的物品。

"副" is a measure word for things that come in pairs.

（1）每年春节的时候，我家都要贴上一副春联。
（2）我有一副红色的手套（shǒutào：glove），很好看。

练 习 | Exercises

判断正误　True (T) or false (F)

（1）汉语里的名词和量词一般要同时用。　　　（　　）

（2）"我"早上吃了一个面包和两片苹果。　　　（　　）

（3）教室的墙上有中国地图和北京地图。　　　（　　）

（4）六节课以后我们去食堂吃饭。　　　　　　（　　）

文化略观 | Cultural Insights

汉语的量词
Measure Words in Chinese

汉语里的量词很多。然而，量词不是毫无规律的。许多量词本身也是名词，比如"瓶"、"杯"，装在瓶子、杯子里的东西就用这些量词。还有，"双"、"对"、"副"等量词一般用于成套的物品，比如鞋、耳环、手套等。另外，有些量词规定了名词的大小、形状，像"条"、"块"、"片"等。知道这些规律后，记忆量词就容易多了。

There are lots of measure words in Chinese. However, there are rules to follow. Many measure words are also nouns in themselves, like "瓶" and "杯". Things contained in them should be accompanied by these measure words. Additionally, there are other measure words like "双", "对" and "副". Generally, they are used for things that come in pairs, like shoes, earrings and gloves. There are some measure words that indicate the size and shape of things, like "条", "块" and "片". Bear these rules in mind, and it will be much easier to remember these measure words.

13

十块钱的自行车
A Ten-Yuan Bike

十块钱能买什么呢?
能买一辆漂亮的自行车! 你相信吗?

拍卖 *n.*
auction

注意 *v.*
notice

Zài yí cì zìxíngchē pāimàihuì shang, yǒu yí gè xiǎo nánháir
在 一 次 自行车 拍卖会 上, 有 一 个 小 男孩儿

zǒngshì chūjià "shí kuài qián", dànshì měi yí cì dōu shì biérén
总是 出价 "十 块 钱", 但是 每 一 次 都 是 别人

yòng yì-liǎngbǎi yuán bǎ zìxíngchē mǎizǒu.
用 一两百 元 把 自行车 买走。

Pāimàihuì zhōngjiān xiūxi shí, pāimàiyuán wèn nàge xiǎo
拍卖会 中间 休息 时, 拍卖员 问 那个 小

nánháir: "Wéishénme bù duō chū yìdiǎnr qián ne?" Nánháir shuō
男孩儿：" 为什么 不 多 出 一点儿 钱 呢？" 男孩儿 说

tā zhǐ yǒu shí kuài qián.
他 只 有 十 块 钱。

Pāimàihuì yòu kāishǐ le, nánháir háishi měi cì zhǐ chū shí
拍卖会 又 开始 了，男孩儿 还是 每 次 只 出 十

kuài qián, ér měi cì dōu shì biérén bǎ zìxíngchē mǎizǒu. Hòulái,
块 钱，而 每 次 都 是 别人 把 自行车 买走。后来，

dàjiā dōu zhùyìdào zhège zǒngshì dì-yī gè chūjià de nánháir.
大家 都 注意到 这个 总是 第一 个 出价 的 男孩儿。

Pāimàihuì mǎshàng yào jiéshù le, zhǐ shèngxia zuì hǎo de yí
拍卖会 马上 要 结束 了，只 剩下 最 好 的 一

liàng zìxíngchē. Pāimàiyuán wèn: "Shuí yào chūjià?" Xiǎo nánháir yòu
辆 自行车。 拍卖员 问："谁 要 出价？" 小 男孩儿 又

shuō: "Shí kuài qián!" Zhè yí cì, méiyǒu rén chū gèng gāo de
说："十 块 钱！" 这 一 次，没有 人 出 更 高 的

jiàqián le. Pāimàiyuán wènle sān cì dōu méiyǒu rén huídá, yúshì
价钱 了。 拍卖员 问了 三 次 都 没有 人 回答，于是

tā dàshēng xuānbù: "Zhè liàng zìxíngchē màigěi zhège xiǎo nánháir!"
他 大声 宣布："这 辆 自行车 卖给 这个 小 男孩儿！"

Zhè shíhou, suǒyǒu de rén dōu zhàn qǐlai gǔzhǎng. Xiǎo
这 时候，所有 的 人 都 站 起来 鼓掌。 小

nánháir náchū shǒu li shī le de shí kuài qián, mǎile nà liàng zuì
男孩儿 拿出 手 里 湿了 的 十 块 钱，买了 那 辆 最

piàoliang de zìxíngchē.
漂亮 的 自行车。

价钱 _n._
price

宣布 _v._
declare

所有 _adj._
all

鼓掌 _v._
applaud

湿 _adj._
wet

想一想 Questions

大家为什么会注意到这个男孩儿？

为什么小男孩儿手里的十块钱是湿的？

语言点 Language Points

总是
always

1. 有一个小男孩儿总是出价"十块钱"。

   There was a boy who always bid the price "ten *yuan*".

   "总是"，副词，表示情况、状态持续不变。

   "总是" is an adverb that indicates a situation or state continues without any change.

   （1）老师讲课的时候总是站着，很辛苦。

   （2）砍树之前，他总是先磨斧子。

剩下
be left, remain

2. 拍卖会马上要结束了，只剩下最好的一辆自行车。

   The auction would be over soon, and only the very best bike was left.

   "剩下"，动词，是去掉一部分之后留下的意思。

   "剩下" is a verb that means to be left as a remainder.

   （1）同学们都走了，教室里只剩下我一个人。

   （2）她有 50 元钱，吃饭 30 元，坐车 10 元，还剩下 10 元钱。

练 习 | Exercises

选择正确答案　Choose the correct answer.

（1）拍卖会上，一辆自行车的价钱一般是（　　）。

　　A. 100~200 元　　　　　B. 1000~2000 元　　　　　C. 10~20 元

（2）拍卖最后一辆自行车时，没有人出比小男孩儿更高的价钱。

　　这是因为（　　）。

　　A. 别人都买到车了　　B. 没人想要那辆车

　　C. 大家想让小男孩儿买到车

（3）小男孩儿买到车时，所有人都站起来鼓掌，是因为（　　）。

　　A. 拍卖会结束了　　　B. 有人买到了便宜的东西

　　C. 人们为小男孩儿感到高兴

文化略观 | Cultural Insights

中国的拍卖业
Auctions in China

　　1986 年，随着第一家国有拍卖行在广州成立，在中国中断了近三十年的拍卖业进入恢复、试点阶段，各类拍卖行如雨后春笋般地出现在中华大地，且逐渐形成规模。1994 年，两大国际拍卖公司——苏富比和佳士得先后在上海设立了办事处，进一步刺激了中国的拍卖业，促进了该行业的迅速发展。

The auction business in China, suspended for nearly 30 years, was restored in 1986. Since the first state-owned auction house was set up in Guangzhou, various auction companies have sprung up all over China and grown into big businesses. In 1994, two international auction companies, Sotheby's and Christie's, opened their offices in Shanghai, which further stimulated the auction business in China and accelerated the rapid development of this industry.

14

"哪里哪里"
"Where, Where?"

中国人学外语、外国人学汉语都会有很多问题。
除了语音、词汇、语法以外，有时候还有文化上的问题。

你全身上下
都很漂亮！

妻子 *n.*
wife

参加 *v.*
attend,
take part in

婚礼 *n.*
wedding ceremony

Yǒu yí gè Yīngguórén, tā zài Zhōngguó shēnghuóle bàn nián,
有 一 个 英国人，他 在 中国 生活了 半 年，

xuéle yìdiǎnr Hànyǔ.
学了 一点儿 汉语。

Yǒu yí cì, zhè wèi xiānsheng hé tā de qīzi yìqǐ cānjiā
有 一 次，这 位 先生 和 他 的 妻子 一起 参加

yí gè Zhōngguó péngyou de hūnlǐ. Hūnlǐ shì zài yì jiā dà fàndiàn
一 个 中国 朋友 的 婚礼。婚礼 是 在 一 家 大 饭店

jǔxíng de. Nà yì tiān, xīnláng hé xīnniáng fēicháng rèqíng. Yīngguó
举行 的。那 一 天， 新郎 和 新娘 非常 热情。 英国

tàitai shì dì-yī cì hé xīnniáng jiànmiàn. Tā wòzhe xīnniáng de
太太 是 第一 次 和 新娘 见面。 她 握着 新娘 的

shǒu, yòng Yīngyǔ duì tā de xiānsheng shuō: "Tā shì wǒ jiànguo
手， 用 英语 对 她 的 先生 说："她 是 我 见过

de zuì piàoliang de Zhōngguó gūniang!" Zhè wèi Yīngguó xiānsheng
的 最 漂亮 的 中国 姑娘！" 这 位 英国 先生

fānyìle zhè jù huà. Xīnláng tīng le, hěn gāoxìng. Tā lǐmào de
翻译了 这 句 话。 新郎 听 了， 很 高兴。 他 礼貌 地

shuō: "Nǎli nǎli."
说："哪里 哪里。"

Yīngguó xiānsheng xué Hànyǔ de shíjiān bù cháng, hái bù
英国 先生 学 汉语 的 时间 不 长， 还 不

zhīdào zhè jù huà shì shénme yìsi, jiù fānyì wéi: "Where,
知道 这 句 话 是 什么 意思， 就 翻译 为："Where,

Where?" Yīngguó tàitai yì tīng, juéde hěn qíguài, xīnxiǎng:
Where?" 英国 太太 一 听， 觉得 很 奇怪， 心想：

zěnme? Hái yào wǒ shuōchū tā nǎr piàoliang ma? Tā bù zhīdào
怎么？ 还 要 我 说出 她 哪儿 漂亮 吗？ 她 不 知道

yīnggāi zěnyàng huídá, zhǐhǎo duì tā zhàngfu shuō: "Nǐ gàosu tā,
应该 怎样 回答， 只好 对 她 丈夫 说："你 告诉 他，

tā de qīzi quánshēn shàng-xià dōu hěn piàoliang."
他 的 妻子 全身 上下 都 很 漂亮。"

举行 *v.*
hold (a meeting, ceremony, etc.)

新郎 *n.*
bridegroom

新娘 *n.*
bride

握手 *v.*
shake hands

礼貌 *adj.*
polite

全身 *n.*
from head to toe, whole body

想一想 Questions

英国先生的汉语怎么样？

"哪里哪里"是什么意思？应该怎么用？

语言点 Language Points

一点儿
some, a little

1. 他在中国生活了半年，学了一点儿汉语。
   He had been living in China for half a year, and had learnt a little Chinese.

   "一点儿"，表示数量很少，修饰名词。

   "一点儿" means "a little". It is used to modify a noun.

   （1）我喝咖啡的时候喜欢放一点儿糖。
   （2）他喝了一点儿水。

是……的
it is … that …

2. 婚礼是在一家大饭店举行的。
   The wedding ceremony was held in a grand hotel.

   "是……的"用来强调与某个已经发生或完成的动作有关的某一方面，如时间、地点、方式等。

   "是……的" is used to emphasize a certain aspect, like time, place or manner, of an action that has happened or finished.

   （1）爸爸是晚上七点回家的。
   （2）玛丽是坐飞机回国的。

练 习 | Exercises

判断正误　True (T) or false (F)

（1）英国先生会说一点儿汉语。　　　　　　　（　　）

（2）英国先生知道 "哪里哪里" 是什么意思。　（　　）

（3）英国先生的翻译是对的。　　　　　　　　（　　）

（4）新郎想知道新娘哪里漂亮。　　　　　　　（　　）

文化略观 | Cultural Insights

不同寻常的 "哪里"
The Unusual "哪里"

　　有些中国话字面上的意思与实际表达的内容不同。比如 "哪里哪里"，实际上表示对别人称赞的一种谦虚，并不是真的询问地点。当你觉得麻烦了别人，表示感谢时，对方也可能会说 "哪儿的话"，也就是 "不用客气"。另外，中国人打招呼有时会问 "你去哪里呀？"，这并不是探究你的隐私，关心你要去哪里，而只是很随意的一种打招呼的方式。你可以含糊地回答 "出去一下" 就行。

The actual meanings of some phrases in Chinese are different from their literal meanings. For example, "哪里哪里" is actually a modest reply to others' compliments, rather than a query about location. When you feel you have bothered someone and have expressed your thanks, the other party may say "哪儿的话", which means "不用客气" (my pleasure). Also, when the Chinese greet each other, they may ask "你去哪里呀？" This does not mean that they want to know where you are going, since this is your own business. It is just a casual way of greeting others, and you can reply vaguely with "出去一下".

15 | 爱因斯坦的小板凳
Einstein's Handiwork

爱因斯坦（Albert Einstein）的第三个小板凳还是不太好看，但已经比前两个小板凳好多了！

笨 *adj.*
stupid

Àiyīnsītǎn zài shàng xiǎoxué de shíhou, lǎoshī hé tóngxué dōu
爱因斯坦 在 上 小学 的 时候，老师 和 同学 都

rènwéi tā shì yí gè hěn bèn de xuésheng. Yǒu yì tiān, lǎoshī
认为 他 是 一 个 很 笨 的 学生。 有 一 天，老师

ràng měi gè rén huíjiā zuò yí jiàn zuòpǐn, dì-èr tiān jiāogěi tā.
让 每 个 人 回家 做 一 件 作品，第二 天 交给 她。

Dì-èr tiān, tóngxuémen dōu dàiláile zìjǐ de zuòpǐn, yǒu

第二 天， 同学们 都 带来了 自己 的 作品，有

wénjùhé, yǒu bùwáwa, hái yǒu hěn duō piàoliang de wánjù. Dāng

文具盒， 有 布娃娃，还 有 很 多 漂亮 的 玩具。 当

Àiyīnsītǎn bǎ zìjǐ de zuòpǐn — yí gè fēicháng nánkàn de

爱因斯坦 把 自己 的 作品 —— 一 个 非常 难看 的

xiǎo bǎndèng jiāogěi lǎoshī de shíhou, jiāoshì li fāchūle cháoxiào

小 板凳 交给 老师 的 时候， 教室 里 发出了 嘲笑

de shēngyīn.

的 声音。

"Ò, Shàngdì, shìjiè shang hái yǒu bǐ zhè gèng nánkàn de

"哦， 上帝， 世界 上 还 有 比 这 更 难看 的

dōngxi ma?" Lǎoshī yáoyao tóu shuō.

东西 吗？" 老师 摇摇 头 说。

"Yǒu." Àiyīnsītǎn yòu náchū liǎng gè gèng nánkàn de xiǎo

"有。"爱因斯坦 又 拿出 两 个 更 难看 的 小

bǎndèng, "Zhè shì dì-yī cì zuò de, zhè shì dì-èr cì zuò de,

板凳， "这 是 第一 次 做 的，这 是 第二 次 做 的，

gāngcái jiāo shàngqu de shì dì-sān cì zuò de. Suīrán bù hǎokàn,

刚才 交 上去 的 是 第三 次 做 的。虽然 不 好看，

dànshì tā bǐ zhè liǎng gè hǎo hěn duō le."

但是 它 比 这 两 个 好 很 多 了。"

Zhèshí, jiàoshì li ānjìngle xiàlái.

这时， 教室 里 安静了 下来。

作品 *n.*
work (of literature
or art)

交 *v.*
hand in

玩具 *n.*
toy

难看 *adj.*
ugly

板凳 *n.*
stool

发出 *v.*
send out (sound,
light, or signals)

嘲笑 *v.*
laugh at, ridicule

上帝 *n.*
God

安静 *adj.*
quiet

想一想 | Questions

老师让每个人回家做什么?

老师觉得爱因斯坦的作品怎么样?

语言点 | Language Points

比
than

1. 世界上还有比这更难看的东西吗?

   Is there anything uglier than this in the world?

   "比",介词,用于比较,它前面和后面的词类或结构常常相同。

   "比" is a preposition used for making comparisons. What comes before and after it are often of the same part of speech or the same structure.

   (1) 新郎比新娘高。

   (2) 肯德基卖的油条比中国饭馆的(油条)贵。

虽然……但是……
although …

2. 虽然不好看,但是它比这两个好很多了。

   Although it does not look nice, it is much better than the other two.

   "虽然……但是……",表示转折关系。"虽然"引导的从句表示承认某种情况为事实。

   "虽然……但是……" indicates transition. "虽然" introduces a clause that acknowledges something as fact.

   (1) 老师虽然快六十了,但是看上去像四十多岁。

   (2) 虽然他才学了半年汉语,但是他已经说得很好了。

练习 Exercises

选择正确答案　Choose the correct answer.

（1）爱因斯坦上小学时，老师和同学认为他（　　）。

　　A. 很聪明　　　　　　　　B. 不聪明　　　　　　　　C. 很难看

（2）文中没有提到的作品是（　　）。

　　A. 布娃娃　　　　　　　　B. 文具盒　　　　　　　　C. 书包

（3）同学们都嘲笑爱因斯坦，因为他的小板凳（　　）。

　　A. 太脏了　　　　　　　　B. 太难看了　　　　　　　C. 太小了

（4）教室里的安静说明大家（　　）。

　　A. 觉得爱因斯坦很努力　　B. 觉得小板凳很难看　　　C. 觉得爱因斯坦很笨

文化略观 Cultural Insights

好孩子是夸出来的
Encouragement Helps Kids Grow

　　鼓励和赞美是教育孩子的重要方式。用这种方式来教育孩子，往往会收到事半功倍的效果。然而，鼓励并不只是简单的表扬。父母需要多发现孩子的优点，多从正面的角度来欣赏和赞美，从而让孩子树立自信。当然，鼓励还要讲究好分寸，把握好尺度，这样才能使家长的有意引导和孩子的自主发展达到和谐统一。所以，如果学会欣赏孩子、鼓励孩子、赞美孩子，那么再普通的孩子也能创造奇迹。

Encouragement and praise are two important ways to educate children. They usually get better results with less effort. However, encouragement does not simply mean praise. Parents should find out more about their children's strong points, and appreciate and praise them to boost their confidence. However, do not go too far in praising them. Only in this way can parents' guidance work in harmony with children's self-development. If you know how to appreciate, encourage and praise your kids, even an ordinary child can create wonders.

16

马的眼睛
The Horse's Eyes

怎样聪明地对付（duìfu: deal with）坏人？
看看张三是怎么做的。

邻居 *n.*
neighbour

偷 *v.*
steal

警察 *n.*
policeman

Yí cì, línjū tōuzǒule Zhāng Sān de mǎ. Zhāng Sān hé
一 次，邻居 偷走了 张 三 的 马。张 三 和

jǐngchá yìqǐ zài línjū de jiāli zhǎodàole mǎ, kěshì línjū bú
警察 一起 在 邻居 的 家里 找到了 马，可是 邻居 不

yuànyì bǎ mǎ jiāo chūlái.
愿意 把 马 交 出来。

Zhāng Sān yòng shǒu bǎ mǎ de shuāngyǎn wǔzhù shuō: "Rúguǒ
张 三 用 手 把 马 的 双眼 捂住 说："如果

zhè mǎ shì nǐ de, nàme, nǐ shuō tā de nǎ zhī yǎnjing shì

这 马 是 你 的，那么，你 说 它 的 哪 只 眼睛 是

xiā de？"

瞎 的？"

"Yòuyǎn." Línjū huídá shuō.

"右眼。"邻居 回答 说。

Zhāng Sān bǎ shǒu cóng yòuyǎn yíkāi, mǎ de yòuyǎn

张 三 把 手 从 右眼 移开，马 的 右眼

yìdiǎnr wèntí dōu méiyǒu.

一点儿 问题 都 没有。

"À, wǒ nòngcuò le," Línjū gǎnmáng shuō, "Shì zuǒyǎn!"

"啊，我 弄错 了，"邻居 赶忙 说，"是 左眼！"

Zhāng Sān bǎ zuǒshǒu yíkāi, mǎ de zuǒyǎn yě méiyǒu

张 三 把 左手 移开，马 的 左眼 也 没有

wèntí.

问题。

"Duìbuqǐ! Wǒ yòu shuōcuò le." Línjū wèi zìjǐ biànhù shuō.

"对不起! 我 又 说错 了。"邻居 为 自己 辩护 说。

"Gòu le gòu le!" Jǐngchá shuō, "Zhè wánquán kěyǐ

"够 了 够 了！"警察 说，"这 完全 可以

zhèngmíng mǎ bú shì nǐ de!"

证明 马 不 是 你 的！"

捂住 *v.*
cover, muffle

瞎 *adj.*
blind

移开 *v.*
remove

辩护 *v.*
defend

想一想 Questions

张三怎么证明邻居偷了他的马？

你觉得张三聪明吗？为什么？

语言点 Language Points

赶忙
hurriedly, hastily

1. "啊，我弄错了，"邻居赶忙说，"是左眼！"

"Ah, I made a mistake," the neighbour said hastily. "It is the left eye!"

"赶忙"，副词，意思是"连忙，很急地"。

"赶忙" is an adverb that means "immediately, anxiously".

（1）听到有人叫她，她赶忙跑出来。

（2）已经八点了，我赶忙起床。

证明
prove, demonstrate

2. 这完全可以证明马不是你的！

This totally proves the horse is not yours!

"证明"，动词，指用证据说明人的身份或事物是真实的，某人的观点、看法等是正确的。

"证明" is a verb that means to prove with evidence the authenticity of one's identity or that a fact, or one's opinion, is correct.

（1）你说你昨天生病了，谁能证明呢？

（2）事实证明我是对的，她说谎了。

练习 Exercises

判断正误　True (T) or false (F)

（1）邻居不知道那匹马是谁的。　　　　　　（　　）

（2）马的一只眼睛看不见东西。　　　　　　（　　）

（3）邻居不知道马的眼睛瞎不瞎。　　　　　（　　）

文化略观 Cultural Insights

马在中国文化中的形象
The Image of the Horse in Chinese Culture

马在中国文化中被赋予了许多正面的品格。首先，马对主人非常忠诚。其次，马能够任劳任怨，忍辱负重，并且非常有战斗力。此外，马还被认为是很有智慧的动物。中国人把那些特别有才能的人称为"千里马"。

The horse is considered a symbol of many good characteristics in the Chinese culture. First, it is very loyal to its master. Second, it can work hard, bear pressure and humiliation, and has a fighting spirit. In addition, the horse is considered a wise animal. The Chinese call people of great talent "千里马" — horses that can cover a thousand *li* (500 metres) a day.

17

午夜电话
A Midnight Call

如果在半夜，你房间的电话突然响了起来，
你会害怕（hàipà：be afraid）吗？

你也是在这个时候，把我从床上折腾起来的。

午夜／半夜 *n.*
midnight

怦 *onomatopoeia*
(of the heart)
thump, pound

接着 *adv.*
then, afterwards

Bànyè li, diànhuà tūrán xiǎngle qǐlai. Xiǎo Lǐ mímíhuhu
半夜 里，电话 突然 响了 起来。小 李 迷迷糊糊
de náqǐ diànhuà, xīn pēngpēng zhí tiào, jiēzhe tā tīngdào: "Shì nǐ
地 拿起 电话，心 怦怦 直 跳，接着 他 听到："是 你
ma, wǒ de háizi?"
吗，我 的 孩子？"

"Ò, māma, shì nǐ. Zěnme le?"
"哦，妈妈，是 你。怎么 了？"

"Méi shénme." Xiǎo Lǐ tīngjiànle māma de xiàoshēng.
"没 什么。" 小 李 听见了 妈妈 的 笑声。

"Wǒ de háizi, jīntiān shì nǐ de shēngrì."
"我 的 孩子，今天 是 你 的 生日。"

"Á? Ài, nǐ bànyè bǎ wǒ cóng chuáng shang jiào qǐlái,
"啊？唉，你 半夜 把 我 从 床 上 叫 起来，

jiù shì wèile gàosu wǒ zhè jiàn shì ma?"
就 是 为了 告诉 我 这 件 事 吗？"

"Sānshí nián qián de jīntiān, nǐ yě shì zài zhège shíhou, bǎ
"三十 年 前 的 今天，你 也 是 在 这个 时候，把

wǒ cóng chuáng shang zhēteng qǐlái de." Māma de yí jù huà bǎ
我 从 床 上 折腾 起来 的。" 妈妈 的 一 句 话 把

Xiǎo Lǐ dòulè le.
小 李 逗乐 了。

Duìyú háizi de shēngrì, jì de zuì qīngchu de rén yéxǔ bú
对于 孩子 的 生日，记 得 最 清楚 的 人 也许 不

shì háizi zìjǐ, ér shì tā de mǔqīn.
是 孩子 自己，而 是 他 的 母亲。

折腾 v.
torture, torment

逗乐 v.
amuse, tickle

对于 prep.
with regard to

想一想 Questions

半夜里发生了
什么事?

你会记住谁的生日?
为什么?

语言点 Language Points

迷迷糊糊
dazed

1. 小李迷迷糊糊地拿起电话。

Xiao Li picked up the phone in a daze.

"迷糊"，形容词，双音节形容词的重叠形式一般是 AABB 式。形容词重叠后，描写作用更强。

"迷糊" is an adjective. Some double-syllable adjectives may follow the reduplication pattern AABB, which can make the description more expressive.

(1) 看到妹妹快快乐乐的样子，我也笑了起来。
(2) 为了漂漂亮亮地过年，很多女孩儿都买了新衣服。

告诉我这件事
tell me this

2. 你半夜把我从床上叫起来，就是为了告诉我这件事吗？

You woke me up in the middle of the night just to tell me this?

有些动词，比如"告诉"、"通知"、"给"、"送"、"交"、"教"等，可以带两个宾语，一个指人，一个指物。指人的宾语放在指物的宾语前面。

Some verbs in Chinese, such as "告诉", "通知", "给", "送", "交", "教" and so on, can have two objects. One refers to a person, and the other refers to something else, which is usually put after the person.

(1) 李老师教我们汉语。
(2) 王太太给小儿子两个苹果。

练 习 Exercises

判断正误　True (T) or false (F)

（1）接到电话，小李的心怦怦直跳，因为他还没有睡醒。　（　　）

（2）小李是在半夜出生的。　（　　）

（3）妈妈给小李打电话，就是为了告诉他今天是他的生日。　（　　）

（4）小李今年三十岁了。　（　　）

文化略观 Cultural Insights

孩子的生日，
母亲的难日

**The Child's Birthday is
the Mother's Suffering Day**

　　中国有句俗话，叫"孩子的生日，母亲的难日"。意思是生孩子对母亲来说是一件十分痛苦的事情。其实，不仅是生孩子这一天，"怀胎十月"，妈妈哪一天不是小心翼翼地度过？所以，中国人过生日的时候一般都要和母亲一起庆祝，以表达对母亲的感谢。

There is a Chinese saying, "The child's birthday is the mother's suffering day." It means that it is very painful for a mother to give birth to a child. Actually, delivery is not the only suffering. Each day of the "ten-month pregnancy" is spent in discomfort and worry. Thus, when celebrating their birthday, Chinese people usually spend it with their mothers to express their gratitude.

18

恋爱日记
A Diary of Her Love

你喜欢旅游吗？旅游的时候遇到过有趣的事情吗？
一起来看看一个女孩儿在旅行中的故事吧。

船长 *n.*
captain (of a ship)

个子 *n.*
height, stature

头发 *n.*
hair

帅 *adj.*
handsome

Dì-yī tiān: Wǒ rènshile chuánzhǎng, tā gèzi gāogāo de,
第一天：我认识了船长，他个子高高的，
tóufa hēihēi de, yǎnjing dàdà de. Tā zhǎng de zhēn shuài!
头发黑黑的，眼睛大大的。他长得真帅！
Dì-èr tiān: Chuánzhǎng qǐng wǒ hé tā yìqǐ chī wǎnfàn.
第二天：船长请我和他一起吃晚饭。
Tā yòu rèqíng yòu yǒu lǐmào, shuōhuà yě hěn yǒuqù, hái gěi wǒ
他又热情又有礼貌，说话也很有趣，还给我
jiǎngle hěn duō xiàohua. Wǒ què xiàng gè shǎguā yíyàng, yí jù huà
讲了很多笑话。我却像个傻瓜一样，一句话

yě shuō bù chūlái.
也 说 不 出来。

Dì-sān tiān: Chuánzhǎng dài wǒ zài chuán shang dàochù
第三 天： 船长 带 我 在 船 上 到处

cānguān, Tā yìzhí shēnqíng de kànzhe wǒ.
参观， 他 一直 深情 地 看着 我。

Dì-sì tiān: Chuánzhǎng zàicì qǐng wǒ chīfàn, wǒmen hái hēle
第四 天： 船长 再次 请 我 吃饭， 我们 还 喝了

diǎnr jiǔ. Hòulái wǒmen yìqǐ qùle tā de fángjiān. Tā shuō tā
点儿 酒。后来 我们 一起 去了 他 的 房间。 他 说 他

ài wǒ, yào hé wǒ jiéhūn. Suīrán wǒ yě xǐhuan tā, kěshì wǒ
爱 我， 要 和 我 结婚。 虽然 我 也 喜欢 他， 可是 我

juéde zhè yíqiè tài kuài le, wǒ hái méi zhǔnbèi hǎo ne. Yúshì wǒ
觉得 这 一切 太 快 了， 我 还 没 准备 好 呢。于是 我

gàosu tā, wǒ yào zài xiǎngxiang.
告诉 他，我 要 再 想想。

Dì-wǔ tiān: Tā yòu shuō yào hé wǒ jiéhūn, hái xiàozhe shuō
第五 天：他 又 说 要 和 我 结婚， 还 笑着 说

rúguǒ wǒ bú yuànyì, tā jiù bǎ chuán zhuàngdào bīngshān shang.
如果 我 不 愿意，他 就 把 船 撞到 冰山 上。

Dì-liù tiān: Wǒ jiùle chuán shang suǒyǒu de rén.
第六 天：我 救了 船 上 所有 的 人。

傻瓜 *n.*
fool

深情 *adj.*
affectionate

一切 *pron.*
all

救 *v.*
save

想一想 Questions

女孩儿喜欢
船长吗?

故事的结果
是什么?

语言点 **Language Points**

参观
visit

1. 船长带我在船上到处参观。

   The captain showed me around the ship.

   "参观"，动词，是到某一个地方观看、观察的意思。

   "参观" is a verb that means to make a visit.

   （1）我们一到北京，老师就带我们参观了这个学校。
   （2）听说你的家很漂亮，我可以参观一下吗？

准备
prepared, ready

2. 我觉得这一切太快了，我还没准备好呢。

   I felt all of these things had happened too fast, and I was not ready yet.

   "准备"，形容词，表示开始做某事之前预先安排好。

   "准备" is an adjective that means to get ready beforehand.

   （1）新年快到了，全家人都在忙着准备新年的礼物。
   （2）我回到家的时候，妈妈已经准备好了饭菜。

练 习　Exercises

选择正确答案　Choose the correct answer.

（1）船长（　　）。

    A. 个子不高　　　　　　B. 头发很黑　　　　　　C. 眼睛很小

（2）"我"没有马上同意和船长结婚，是因为（　　）。

    A. "我"还没准备好　　　B. "我"不喜欢船长　　　C. 船长喝酒喝多了

（3）"我救了船上所有的人"的意思是（　　）。

    A. "我"同意和船长结婚　　B. 船撞到了冰山，"我"去救人了

    C. "我"同意和船长一起吃饭

文化略观　Cultural Insights

郑和下西洋
Zheng He's Voyages

郑和是中国历史上伟大的航海家。公元 1405 年，郑和奉明成祖朱棣之命，开始了他七次伟大的航海旅程，称为"下西洋"。郑和率领船队出使东南亚、南亚，最远去到东非，在外交、军事和贸易方面取得了很多成就。

郑和的船队去过马来群岛、泰国、印度、阿拉伯和东非。他们带去了来自中国的礼物，例如黄金、丝绸和瓷器。他们也带回了很多奇珍异宝，包括象牙、骆驼和中国的第一只长颈鹿。

郑和为世界航海事业的发展和各国人民的交流作出了不可磨灭的贡献。

Zheng He was a great explorer in Chinese history. In 1405, he was sent by the Ming emperor Zhu Di on the first of his seven great voyages, called the "Voyages to the Western Seas", travelling to South-East Asia, South Asia and as far afield as East Africa in expeditions during which Zheng He accrued many diplomatic, military and trading accomplishments.

Zheng He's fleets visited the Malay Archipelago, Thailand, India, Arabia and East Africa. They presented gifts from China such as gold, silk and porcelain. They brought back many valuable and novel things, including ivory, camels, and the first giraffe in China.

Zheng He made great contributions to the development of world navigation and communication between people of different countries.

19 伤心的故事

A Sad Story

三个好朋友住在饭店的 35 层。电梯坏了，只好一起爬楼梯。
大家一边爬，一边讲笑话、唱歌，最后一个人讲了个故事……

糟糕 *adj.*
bad, terrible

电梯 *n.*
lift

楼梯 *n.*
stairs

Yǒu sān gè rén dào Nánjīng lǚyóu, tāmen zhù zài yí gè
有 三 个 人 到 南京 旅游，他们 住 在 一 个

fàndiàn de 35 céng. Wǎnshang tāmen yìqǐ chūqù kàn diànyǐng,
饭店 的 35 层。 晚上 他们 一起 出去 看 电影，

huílái de shíhou yǐjīng hěn wǎn le. Zāogāo de shì, suǒyǒu de
回来 的 时候 已经 很 晚 了。糟糕 的 是，所有 的

diàntī dōu huài le, tāmen zhǐhǎo zìjǐ zǒu shàngqu.
电梯 都 坏 了，他们 只好 自己 走 上去。

Tāmen kāishǐ pá lóutī.　Yí gè rén shuō:"Wǒmen zhèyàng zǒu
他们　开始　爬　楼梯。一　个　人　说:"我们　　这样　　走

tài wúliáo le.　Zhèyàng ba, wǒmen yí gè rén jiǎng xiàohua, yí gè
太　无聊　了。　这样　吧,　我们　一　个　人　讲　笑话,　一　个

rén chànggē, yí　gè rén jiǎng gùshi."
人　唱歌,　一　个　人　讲　故事。"

Dàjiā dōu juéde hěn hǎo. Tāmen jìxù pá lóutī,　yí gè rén
大家　都　觉得　很　好。他们　继续　爬　楼梯,　一　个　人

jiǎngle xiàohua, ránhòu dì-èr gè rén chàngle gē. Dào 25 céng de
讲了　笑话,　然后　第二　个　人　唱了　歌。到 25　层　的

shíhou, dàjiā dōu lèi le,　juédìng xiān xiūxi yíxià.
时候,大家　都　累　了,　决定　先　休息　一下。

Jiǎng xiàohua de rén duì dì-sān gè rén shuō:"Wǒ jiǎngle
讲　笑话　的　人　对　第三　个　人　说:"我　讲了

xiàohua, tā chàngle gē, xiànzài gāi nǐ jiǎng gùshi le.　Nǐ yào jiǎng
笑话,　他　唱了　歌,　现在　该　你　讲　故事　了。你　要　讲

yí gè cháng yìdiǎnr de gùshi, zuìhǎo yǒu yí gè shāngxīn de
一　个　长　一点儿　的　故事,　最好　有　一　个　伤心　的

jiéwěi."
结尾。"

Dì-sān gè rén shuō:"Wǒ xiànzài jiù jiǎng yí gè shāngxīn de
第三　个　人　说:"我　现在　就　讲　一　个　伤心　的

gùshi, gùshi bù cháng, dàn hěn ràng rén shāngxīn — wǒmen de
故事,故事　不　长,　但　很　让　人　伤心——我们　的

fángjiān yàoshi wàng zài yī lóu fúwùtái le."
房间　钥匙　忘　在　一　楼　服务台　了。"

无聊 *adj.*
boring

休息 *v.*
rest

最好 *adv.*
had better

结尾 *n.*
ending

钥匙 *n.*
key

服务台 *n.*
service counter

想一想 Questions

他们为什么要爬楼梯?

故事的结尾让人伤心吗?

语言点 Language Points

一下
for a short while,
have a try

1. 到 25 层的时候，大家都累了，决定先休息一下。
   Having reached the 25th floor, everybody was exhausted, and they decided to have a rest.

   "一下"，放在动词后面，表示动作持续时间短。
   "一下" is usually put after a verb to indicate that the action only has a short duration.

   （1）下课的时候应该出去活动一下，休息休息。
   （2）你敲一下门，看看里面有没有人。

该
it is one's
turn to do
something

2. 我讲了笑话，他唱了歌，现在该你讲故事了。
   I have told a joke, he has sung a song, and now it is your turn to tell a story.

   "该"表示应该轮到某人做某事。后面常加"了"，但否定的时候一般不加。
   "该" means it is one's turn to do something. It is often used with "了" at the end. But there is no "了" in a negative sentence.

   （1）五点了，该放学了。
   （2）今天不该他休息，他怎么没来上班?

练 习 | **Exercises**

判断正误　True (T) or false (F)

(1) 这三个人住在上海一家饭店的 35 层。 （　　）

(2) 走到 15 层的时候，大家决定休息一下。 （　　）

(3) 第三个人讲故事之前，就发现没带钥匙。 （　　）

文化略观 | **Cultural Insights**

"马大哈" 的由来
The Origin of "马大哈"

　　"马大哈" 是指做事马马虎虎的人。这个词来自相声《买猴》。一位叫 "马大哈" 的干部，以马虎出名。他写了个购货单，本来要通知 "到天津市的东北角，买猴牌肥皂五十箱"，可是错写成了 "到东北买猴五十只"。结果，采购员跑遍了大半个中国去采购猴子。猴子运回来以后，群猴出笼大闹百货公司……

　　The term "马大哈" refers to those who are careless about their work or life. It came from a comic Chinese dialogue called *Buying Monkeys*. Ma Daha, a manager of a department store, was well known for his carelessness. He made a shopping list with the intention of having his purchasing man "go to the northeast corner of Tianjin and buy 50 boxes of Monkey-brand soap". However, by mistake he wrote "go to the Northeast and buy 50 monkeys". As a result, the purchasing man travelled across half the country to buy monkeys. When the 50 monkeys were brought in, they all escaped from the cages and ran amok in the store ...

20

最好的消息
The Best News

如果你知道一个人欺骗〔qīpiàn：deceive〕了你，
你会不会生气？

> 我的孩子
> 病得快死了……

赢 v.
win

比赛 n.
game, match

可怜 adj.
poor

感动 v.
move

　　Yí gè zhùmíng de yùndòngyuán yíngle yì chǎng zhòngyào
一个 著名 的 运动员 赢了 一 场 重要

de bǐsài, dédàole hěn duō jiǎngjīn. Bǐsài jiéshù hòu, tā zhǔnbèi
的 比赛，得到了 很 多 奖金。比赛 结束 后，他 准备

huíjiā. Zhè shíhou, yí gè niánqīng de nǚzǐ xiàng tā zǒulái. Tā
回家。这 时 候，一 个 年轻 的 女子 向 他 走来。她

xiān xiàng yùndòngyuán biǎoshì zhùhè, ránhòu jiù gàosu tā, tā
先 向 运动员 表示 祝贺，然后 就 告诉 他，她

kělián de háizi bìng de hěn zhòng, yěxǔ huì sǐ, ér tā què méi
可怜 的 孩子 病 得 很 重， 也许 会 死，而 她 却 没

qián gěi tā kànbìng.
钱 给 他 看病。

Yùndòngyuán bèi tā de huà shēnshēn de gǎndòng le. Tā
运动员 被 她 的 话 深深 地 感动 了。他

xiǎngle xiǎng, náchū bǐ zài gāng yíngdé de zhīpiào shang fēikuài de
想了 想, 拿出 笔 在 刚 赢得 的 支票 上 飞快 地

qiānle míng, ránhòu bǎ zhīpiào gěile nàge nǚzǐ.
签了 名, 然后 把 支票 给了 那个 女子。

"Zhè shì bǐsài jiǎngjīn. Zhù kělián de háizi hǎoyùn." Tā shuō.
"这 是 比赛 奖金。 祝 可怜 的 孩子 好运。"他 说。

Yí gè xīngqī hòu, yùndòngyuán zhèngzài yì jiā fàndiàn chīfàn.
一 个 星期 后, 运动员 正在 一 家 饭店 吃饭。

Fàndiàn lǎobǎn wèn tā, yì zhōu qián shì bú shì yùdàoguo yí gè
饭店 老板 问 他, 一 周 前 是 不 是 遇到过 一 个

niánqīng nǚzǐ, shuō zìjǐ de háizi bìng de hěn zhòng.
年轻 女子, 说 自己 的 孩子 病 得 很 重。

Tā diǎnle diǎn tóu.
他 点 了 点 头。

"Ò, duì nǐ lái shuō zhè shì gè huài xiāoxi." Lǎobǎn
"哦, 对 你 来 说 这 是 个 坏 消息。"老板

shuō, "Nàge nǚrén shì gè piànzi, tā gēnběn jiù méiyǒu shénme
说,"那个 女人 是 个 骗子, 她 根本 就 没有 什么

bìng de hěn zhòng de háizi. Tā hái méiyǒu jiéhūn ne!"
病 得 很 重 的 孩子。她 还 没有 结婚 呢!"

"Nǐ shì shuō gēnběn jiù méiyǒu yí gè xiǎo háizi bìng de
"你 是 说 根本 就 没有 一 个 小 孩子 病 得

kuài sǐ le?"
快 死 了?"

"Shì zhèyàng de, gēnběn jiù méiyǒu."
"是 这样 的, 根本 就 没有。"

"Shì ma? Zhè zhēn shì wǒ tīngdào de zuì hǎo de xiāoxi!"
"是 吗? 这 真 是 我 听到 的 最 好 的 消息!"

支票 *n.*
cheque

签名 *v.*
sign one's name

好运 *n.*
fortune, good luck

消息 *n.*
news

骗子 *n.*
cheat, fraud

想一想 **Questions**

年轻的女子想干什么?

你觉得这是个好消息还是坏消息?为什么?

语言点 **Language Points**

祝贺
congratulate

1. 她先向运动员表示祝贺,然后就告诉他,她可怜的孩子病得很重。

First she congratulated the sportsman, and then told him that her poor child was seriously ill.

"祝贺",动词,表示在对方取得成功或有喜事时,用语言向对方表示庆祝。

"祝贺" is a verb meaning to express congratulations in words when someone has achieved success or something nice has happened.

(1) 我生日的时候,很多同学向我表示祝贺。

(2) 祝贺你这次考试取得了第一名!

祝
wish

2. 祝可怜的孩子好运。

Wish the poor child good luck.

"祝",动词,表示对人或事情表达良好的愿望。

"祝" is a verb used to express good wishes to somebody or something.

(1) 马上就要出发了,祝你们一路平安!

(2) 祝你生日快乐!

练习 | Exercises

选择正确答案　Choose the correct answer.

(1) 运动员在支票上签了名，是因为（　　）。

A. 女子向他要一个签名　　B. 女子的孩子很喜欢他　　C. 这样女子才能拿到钱

(2) 运动员把比赛的奖金送给女子，因为（　　）。

A. 他认识那个女子　　B. 她的孩子生病了　　C. 他的奖金不多

(3) 那个女子是个骗子，运动员却觉得这是个好消息，因为（　　）。

A. 骗子的钱还可以要回来　　B. 他给的钱不太多　　C. 没有一个生病的孩子

文化略观 | Cultural Insights

名人的慈善行动
Celebrity Charity Action

现在，越来越多的中国企业家和明星开始具有了慈善意识。这不是一个简单的时尚行为。慈善事业既有利于树立他们自身良好的形象，也会有利于一些企业家事业的发展。更重要的是，这样做能够让普通人多一些慈善意识。2008 年 5 月 12 日四川发生大地震后，功夫明星李连杰发起的"中国红十字会李连杰壹基金计划"就和很多普通人一起，共同努力，给灾区人民送去了很多帮助。

Nowadays, more and more entrepreneurs and stars in China have become aware of the importance of charity. This is not just a simple fad, but an undertaking that helps to establish a favourable public image of these entrepreneurs and stars, which, in turn, helps their career development. More importantly, their examples also help to promote charity awareness among the general public. After an earthquake occurred on 12 May 2008 in Sichuan, kung fu star Jet Li (Li Lianjie) initiated the "Red Cross China Jet Li One Foundation Project", which worked together with many ordinary people in the relief efforts to help earthquake victims.

1 The Blind Man's Lantern

There was a blind man who always carried a bright lantern with him when going out in the evening. One person found this very odd and asked him, "Since you can't see, why do you carry a lantern while walking?"

Smiling, the blind man said, "I can't see myself, but my lantern can light the way for others."

"Why does lighting the way for others have anything to do with you?"

The blind man said, "I use the lantern not to light my way, but for others to see me. This way, they will not bump into me."

2 Pronouncing Chinese

Pronouncing Chinese is a little difficult. Why is that?

Firstly, because there are four tones in Chinese. Non-Chinese speakers feel it is difficult to learn tones, and often make fools of themselves. One day, a foreigner could not find the supermarket he wanted to go to. He saw a pretty lady beside him and said, "Miss, I have a question. May I ask you?" The lady heard this and got angry. Do you know why? Because the foreigner had pronounced "wèn (问)" as "wěn (吻, meaning kiss)". Apart from the tones, the rhotic accent is also not easy. For example, you should say "小孩儿 (xiǎoháir) instead of "小孩 (xiǎohái).

Secondly, retroflex sounds are very difficult. For example, some foreign students say "我是 (sì) 美国人" instead of "我是 (shì) 美国人". What's more, many people cannot clearly distinguish between "四 (sì)" and "十 (shí)". So, in class, our teacher has us say: 四是四，十是十，十四是十四，四十是四十 (sì shì sì, shí shì shí; shísì shì shísì, sìshí shì sìshí).

3 The Meaning of "好"

Ms Zhang: Everyone think for a moment: why is the character "好" composed of "女" and "子" together?

Student A: The word "女子" means girls. If you have a girlfriend, it is good.

Student B: No, you're wrong. "女" means daughters, while "子" stands for sons. It is good to have both daughters (女) and sons (子).

Student C: You're wrong, too. "女" means "girls" while "子" stands for "boys". It is good (好) for girls (女) and boys (子) to be together. In our class, girls and boys learn Chinese together. That's very good!

Ms Zhang: What your classmates have said is all very interesting. From now on, think things over a little more when learning Chinese characters and you will memorize them easily.

4 Poor Monk, Rich Monk

Once upon a time, there were two monks, one very rich and the other very poor.

One day, the poor monk said to the rich monk, "I'd like to go to India to study the Buddhist scriptures. What do you think?"

The rich monk said, "The road is too long. How will you get there?"

The poor monk said, "I have one bowl, one cup and two feet. That's enough, isn't it?"

When the rich monk heard this he burst out laughing, and said, "I've wanted to go to India for years, but I've never been there, because I don't have enough money. You are so poor, how can you manage to get there?"

Three years later, the poor monk returned from India and brought a Buddhist scripture back for the rich monk. The rich monk felt very ashamed.

5 Bargaining

Buying things in China is very different. That is because you can haggle.

The following is a bargaining conversation I had yesterday:

Shopkeeper: This item of clothing looks very good. Try it on!

Me: How much is it?

Shopkeeper: Not expensive, 160 yuan.

Me: What? Too expensive!

Shopkeeper: How much would you say?

Me: 100 yuan.

Shopkeeper: Well, that's too low, no.

Me: Then I'm leaving.

Shopkeeper: Ah, wait a minute, what about 130?

Me: 130 is too much. I am a student, I don't have money.

Shopkeeper: What's the highest price you can give?

Me: 100 yuan.

Shopkeeper: OK, let's make a compromise, what about 120 yuan?

Me: Fine.

Shopkeeper: Here you are. Please come again.

6 Bicycle Kingdom

Because the number of cyclists is so great, some people call China the "kingdom of bicycles".

In Chinese cities during rush hour, bikes flow like the tide down the streets. One bicycle costs just a few hundred yuan, which is very cheap, so in many Chinese families, each person has a bike. In China, some university campuses are very large, so many university students also have bikes.

In the U.S. and Europe, people often cycle for exercise, whereas in China bikes are mainly a means of transport. Bicycles are extremely environmentally friendly, and have many advantages. However, in recent years, there have been more and more cars in China, and the traffic jams in big cities have got more and more severe. If only China can continue to be a "bicycle kingdom".

7 Sightseeing or Photographing?

There is a very interesting picture, which tells everyone that when they go travelling, the behaviour of Chinese people and westerners is quite different. There is an eye on the right of the picture, representing westerners. Its meaning is that when westerners travel, they like to use their own eyes to appreciate the scenery. On the left of the picture is a camera, representing the Chinese. Its meaning is that when Chinese people travel, they like to bring a camera everywhere to take pictures.

Indeed, in the past, Chinese people had very few opportunities to travel, and chances to go travelling outside the country were even fewer. As a result, many people liked to use their cameras instead of their eyes. They would take pictures non-stop, and when they came home, they would look at the photographs and think back on the places they had been. Following China's economic development, more and more Chinese people are beginning to travel abroad. People are also increasingly realizing that, although looking at photos and reminiscing is important, it is more important to use your own eyes to appreciate the scenery in front of you.

8 Funny Drunks

A father and a son were both drunkards. They liked drinking very much and often got drunk.

One day, the father went out and got very drunk. He stumbled back to the apartment building where they lived. They lived on the third floor, but he knocked on a door on the second floor. Without opening the door, the person on the second floor shouted out: "Your home is upstairs!" The father returned home with great difficulty. After he got inside, he stared at his son's face for a while and said angrily: "So weird, why do you have three faces? You are a weird thing. I definitely won't leave my house to you!" His son had also got very drunk at home. Upon hearing his father's words, he did not take kindly to them and said: "That would be better! A house that sways like this? Even if you gave it to me, I wouldn't accept it!"

9 Whet the Axe

There was a young lumberjack who, with great difficulty, got a job with very good working conditions. He liked his job very much, and was determined to do it well.

On the first day, he cut down 18 trees. The boss was very happy and encouraged him: "Well done!" The young worker felt very pleased.

On the second day, though he kept working, he cut down only 15 trees.

On the third day, he still worked very, very hard, but he cut down only 10 trees.

The worker felt so ashamed that he apologized to the boss. "I don't know why. I worked very hard, but my strength is failing."

The boss asked him, "When did you last whet your axe?"

"Whet the axe?" the worker suddenly realized. "I was busy cutting down trees every day, but I forgot to whet the axe!"

10 Taxis in Beijing

It is very convenient to take a taxi in Beijing. The starting price is 10 *yuan* for the first three kilometres. From then on, the price is 2 *yuan* per kilometre. For example, it is more than 40 kilometres from the airport to Peking University and costs approximately 100 *yuan*.

Beijingers usually call taxis "的士" or "出租" and taking a taxi is called "打的" or "打车". Beijing taxi drivers are affectionately called "的哥" or "的姐", although these are seldom used to their faces. Face to face, "师傅" is usually used. Beijing taxi drivers are great fun. They like chatting with you and if there's anything you don't know, just ask them. They are very warm-hearted and willing to answer all kinds of questions.

In addition, when you are taking a taxi, do remember two things: first, do not forget your belongings; and second, get in and out through the right-hand door.

11 The Chimp that Quit Smoking

Feifei is a chimpanzee at the zoo. He is very lovable. However, tourists in the zoo often threw cigarette butts at him. Feifei gradually started smoking too. He smoked more and more, even to the point of ten cigarettes a day, sometimes.

Because he was smoking too much, Feifei became increasingly fragile. In spring, Feifei caught a cold several times, and even got pneumonia.

The staff of the zoo made a plan to make Feifei quit smoking. In the beginning, the staff gave him ten cigarettes a day, then eight, then five... fewer and fewer. When Feifei wanted to smoke, the staff gave him milk. They also told visitors not to give any more cigarettes to Feifei.

Two months later, Feifei successfully quit smoking.

12 Measure Words and Nouns

Chinese measure words are often put in front of nouns. Measure words and nouns are inseparable. Take a look at a day in my life and you will see.

I got up at 7:30 a.m. First I went into the kitchen, drank a bottle of milk, ate three slices of bread and an apple, and then went back to the bedroom. I put on a coat and a pair of shoes. I carried a satchel (containing three books, two pens and a mobile phone) on my back to college.

On the way, I saw an adorable puppy. When I reached the classroom, I noticed a map of China newly put up on the wall. When the class was about to begin, a teacher came in. He wore a pair of glasses. After four classes, we went to the canteen to eat. I ordered a bottle of beer and a serving of stir-fried eggs with tomatoes.

13 A Ten-Yuan Bike

At a bicycle auction, there was a boy who always bid the price "ten *yuan*", but each time, someone else bought the bike for around one or two hundred *yuan*.

During a break, the auctioneer asked the boy, "Why didn't you make a higher offer?" The boy said that he had only ten *yuan*.

The auction resumed. The boy still only bid ten *yuan* every time, and each time the bike was bought by someone else. As time went on, everyone at the auction noticed the boy, who had always been the first to bid.

The auction would be over soon, and only the very best bike was left. The auctioneer asked, "Who would like to bid?" The boy said again, "Ten *yuan*!" This time, nobody made a higher offer. The auctioneer asked three times, but still nobody answered. Then he declared loudly, "The bicycle is sold to this boy!"

Then everyone stood up and applauded. The boy took out the wet and sweaty ten-*yuan* note from his hand, and bought the very best bike.

14 Where, Where?

There was a man from Britain. He had been living in China for half a year, and had learnt a little Chinese.

Once, this man and his wife attended a Chinese friend's wedding ceremony. The wedding ceremony was held in a grand hotel. That day, the bridegroom and the bride were very cordial. This was the first time that the British wife had met the bride. Shaking hands with the bride, she said to her husband in English, "She is the prettiest Chinese girl I have ever seen!" The British husband translated the sentence. Upon hearing this, the bridegroom was very happy and replied politely, "哪里哪里".

Having not studied Chinese for long, the British husband did not know what this meant. So he translated it as "Where, where?" The British wife found this very strange and thought to herself: What? Do I need to say where she is beautiful? Not knowing how she ought to reply, she had no choice but to say to her husband, "Just tell him his wife is very pretty from head to toe."

15 Einstein's Handiwork

In primary school, Einstein was considered a very stupid student by his teachers and his classmates. One day, the teacher told everyone to make a piece of craftwork at home and hand it in to her the next day.

The next day, the whole class brought their work, which included writing cases, cloth dolls and many beautiful toys. However, when Einstein handed in his work, a very ugly little wooden stool, to the teacher, the whole class burst into laughter.

"Oh, Lord, is there anything uglier than this in the world?" said the teacher, shaking her head.

"Yes, there is." Einstein took out two even uglier little stools, "This was made first and this second. The one I handed in just now is the third. Although it does not look nice, it is much better than the other two."

At that moment, the classroom suddenly went quiet.

16 The Horse's Eyes

Once, a neighbour stole Zhang San's horse. Zhang San went with a policeman and found the horse at the neighbour's house, but the neighbour was not willing to hand it over.

Zhang San covered the horse's eyes with his hands and said, "If this horse is yours, then tell us, which eye is the blind one?"

"The right," said the neighbour.

Zhang San removed his hand from the right eye. There was nothing wrong with the horse's right eye at all.

"Ah, I made a mistake," the neighbour said hastily. "It is the left eye!"

Zhang San removed his hand from the left eye. There was nothing wrong with the horse's left eye either.

"Sorry, I misspoke again!" said the neighbour, to defend himself.

"Enough, enough!" said the policeman. "This totally proves the horse is not yours!"

17 A Midnight Call

At midnight, the phone suddenly rang. Xiao Li picked up the phone in a daze, his heart pounding hard, and then he heard, "Is that you, my child?"

"Oh, it's you, Mum. What's the matter?"

"Nothing really." Xiao Li heard his mother's laughter. "My child, today is your birthday."

"What? Ah, you woke me up in the middle of the night just to tell me this?"

"Thirty years ago today, it was also at this time when you tortured me out of bed." Xiao Li was amused by his mother's words.

When it comes to a child's birthday, the one who remembers it most clearly may be his mother rather than the child himself.

18 A Diary of Her Love

Day One: I met the captain. He is tall, has black hair and big eyes. He is so handsome!

Day Two: The captain invited me to have dinner with him. He was friendly and polite. His conversation was interesting too and he told me a lot of jokes. But like a fool, I said barely a word.

Day Three: The captain showed me around the ship. He looked at me affectionately all along.

Day Four: The captain invited me for dinner again. We also had some drinks. Later we went to his cabin together. He said he loved me and wanted to marry me. Though I also like him, I felt all of these things had happened too fast, and I was not ready yet. So I told him I had to think it over.

Day Five: He said again that he wanted to marry me and, smiling, he said if I did not agree, he would drive the ship into an iceberg.

Day Six: I saved everyone aboard ship.

19 A Sad Story

Three people were visiting Nanjing and were staying on the 35th floor of a hotel. In the evening, they went out to see a film and returned to the hotel very late. Unfortunately, all the lifts were out of order, so they had no choice but to walk up.

They began to climb the stairs. One person said, "It is too boring to just walk. How about this? One of us tells a joke, one sings a song and one tells a story?"

All thought it was a very good idea. They continued up the stairs. One person told a joke, and then another sang a song. Having reached the 25th floor, everybody was exhausted, and they decided to have a rest.

The person who had told a joke said to the third person, "I have told a joke, he has sung a song, and now it is your turn to tell a story. You should tell a story that's long, and you had better give it a sad ending."

The third person said, "Now I am going to tell a sad story, which is not long, but very sad — we left our room key on the first-floor service counter."

20 The Best News

A famous sportsman won an important competition and got a lot of prize money. After the contest, he got ready to go home. Just then a young lady came over to him. First she congratulated the sportsman, and then told him that her poor child was seriously ill, and might even die, but she had no money for the child to see a doctor.

The sportsman was deeply moved by her words. He thought for a while, took out a pen and signed his name like a shot on the cheque he had just won. Then he handed the cheque over to the woman.

"This is the prize money. Wish the poor child good luck," he said.

One week later, the sportsman was having dinner in a restaurant. The restaurant owner asked him whether he had come across a young lady one week before, who had said that her child had been seriously ill.

He nodded.

"Well, this may be a piece of bad news for you," the owner said. "That woman is a fraud. She does not have any seriously sick child at all. She is not even married!"

"Do you mean that there wasn't a child ill and on the verge of death at all?"

"Yes, I do. None at all."

"Really? This is indeed the best news that I have ever heard!"

练习答案
Answer Key

1.   F, F, T

2.   T, F, T

3.   F, F, T

4.   F, F, T, T

5.   B, C, B

6.   F, T, T, F

7.   T, T, T, T

8.   C, C, A

9.   C, B, C, B

10. F, T, T, T

11. F, T, F, T

12. T, F, F, F

13. A, C, C

14. T, F, F, F

15. B, C, B, A

16. F, F, T

17. F, T, T, T

18. B, A, A

19. F, F, T

20. C, B, C